flip
this
school

how to
lead the
turnaround
process

JOHN F. ELLER & SHEILA A. ELLER

Solution Tree | Press

a division of
Solution Tree

555 North Morton Street

Bloomington, IN 47404

800.733.6786 (toll free) / 812.336.7700

FAX: 812.336.7790

email: info@SolutionTree.com

SolutionTree.com

Visit **go.SolutionTree.com/schoolimprovement** to download the free reproducibles in this book.

Printed in the United States of America

Library of Congress Cataloging-in-Publication Data

Names: Eller, John, 1957- author. | Eller, Sheila, author.
Title: Flip this school : how to lead the turnaround process / John F. Eller
    and Sheila A. Eller.
Description: Bloomington, IN : Solution Tree Press, [2019] | Includes
    bibliographical references and index.
Identifiers: LCCN 2018053764 | ISBN 9781936765447 (perfect bound)
Subjects: LCSH: School improvement programs--United States. | Educational
    change--United States. | School management and organization--United States.
Classification: LCC LB2822.82 .E543 2019 | DDC 371.2/07--dc23 LC record available at https://lccn.
loc.gov/2018053764

Solution Tree
Jeffrey C. Jones, CEO
Edmund M. Ackerman, President

Solution Tree Press
President and Publisher: Douglas M. Rife
Associate Publisher: Sarah Payne-Mills
Art Director: Rian Anderson
Managing Production Editor: Kendra Slayton
Senior Production Editor: Suzanne Kraszewski
Content Development Specialist: Amy Rubenstein
Copy Editor: Kate St. Ives
Proofreader: Elisabeth Abrams
Text and Cover Designer: Jill Resh
Editorial Assistant: Sarah Ludwig

Acknowledgments

Solution Tree Press would like to thank the following reviewers:

Jennifer Perkins
Assistant Principal
Center Grove High School
Greenwood, Indiana

Akil E. Ross
Founder, HeartEd LLC
2018 NASSP National Principal of the Year
Chapin High School
Chapin, South Carolina

Christopher Snyder
Principal
Daniel J. Bakie Elementary School
Kingston, New Hampshire

Visit **go.SolutionTree.com/schoolimprovement** to download the free reproducibles in this book.

Table of Contents

Chapter 4

Assessing and Developing Your Leadership Skills 67

Chapter 5

Gathering Data About Your School 85

Chapter 6

Obtaining Commitment From the District 117

Chapter 7

Maintaining a Positive and Productive Culture 133

About the Authors

John F. Eller, PhD is a former principal, director of a principal's training center, and assistant superintendent for curriculum, learning, and staff development.

John specializes in school turnaround, dealing with difficult people, building professional learning communities, conducting employee evaluations, building conferencing and coaching skills, developing strategic planning strategies, recruiting employees, selecting and inducting employees, building supervisory skills, and implementing effective teaching strategies. He has served as executive director of the Minnesota Association for Supervision and Curriculum Development (ASCD). He has written articles for the Master Teacher publication *Superintendents Only*, authored *Effective Group Facilitation in Education: How to Energize Meetings and Manage Difficult Groups*, and coauthored *Working With and Evaluating Difficult School Employees*, *So Now You're the Superintendent!*, *Energizing Staff Meetings*, *Creative Strategies to Transform School Culture*, *Thriving as a New Teacher*, *Score to Soar*, *Achieving Great Impact*, and *Working With Difficult and Resistant Staff*.

John earned a doctorate in educational leadership and policy studies from Loyola University Chicago and a master's degree in educational leadership from the University of Nebraska Omaha.

Sheila A. Eller, EdD, is a middle school principal for the Mounds View Public Schools in Minnesota. She has served as a principal in Fairfax County (Virginia) Public Schools and other schools in Minnesota. Sheila is a former principal, university professor, special education teacher, Title I mathematics teacher, and self-contained classroom teacher for grades 1–4.

In Fairfax County, Sheila helped transform a school that was not making adequate yearly progress, had low socioeconomic status, and had a high minority population through professional learning community implementation, data use, and refinement of teaching and learning strategies.

Sheila shares her expertise at international conferences and with school districts in the areas of school turnaround, effective instruction, teacher evaluation, instructional leadership teams, teacher leadership, and various other topics. As a professor at National Louis University in Chicago, she worked on the development team for a classroom mathematics series, and her teaching skills were featured on a video that accompanied the series. She has coauthored *Energizing Staff Meetings*, *Working With and Evaluating Difficult School Employees*, *Creative Strategies to Transform School Culture*, *Thriving as a New Teacher*, *Score to Soar*, *Achieving Great Impact*, and *Working With Difficult and Resistant Staff*.

She has been a member of the Minnesota ASCD executive board and a regional president of the Minnesota Elementary School Principals' Association.

Sheila received a doctorate in educational leadership and administration from St. Cloud State University, a master's degree from Creighton University, and a bachelor's degree from Iowa State University.

To learn more about John and Sheila's work, visit www.ellerandassociates.com or follow @jellerthree on Twitter.

To book John Eller or Sheila Eller for professional development, contact pd@SolutionTree.com.

Preface

If you're reading this book, you have decided to take on the task of turning around the performance of a school. You might be new to your leadership role or school, or you might have many years of experience in a school in which you are very invested. Either way, your work will have a major impact on children and families in your school community. We have seen this positive impact happen in schools we have supported or ourselves worked to turn around. This positive impact is the reward that makes all of the hard work worthwhile.

In this book, we share processes, strategies, tools, and stories compiled from many sources; some information is based in educational research, while other information we share is based on our experiences with school turnaround, both in schools in which we have been leaders and those we have supported through the turnaround process. In assisting other leaders, we have learned how their turnaround projects had to be tailored to meet the specific conditions of their schools. Most of the information contained in this book comes from our own personal experiences in turning around schools. These experiences gave us the opportunity to understand what works as well as what is not as effective, and what challenges can emerge.

You'll notice in this book there are many stories and examples of principals working on different aspects of the turnaround process. These stories are based on our own personal experiences or the experiences of principals we have worked with over the years. We changed the names, genders, levels, and other identifying characteristics in these stories to ensure anonymity of those involved in the original situations. These stories will help you see the processes and strategies we explain in this book in action.

This book is written from the perspective of a principal, director, or other school leader, but the strategies and ideas we present can be used by teacher instructional leadership teams, instructional improvement team members, superintendents, and many others charged with the task of improving schools to benefit student learning.

Each school-turnaround project is different. What works in one situation may not work in another. You may need to make changes and adjustments based on your unique situation and the needs of your school. Keeping this in mind will help you as you tailor the work for your turnaround project.

We know you will find the ideas and strategies we provide here helpful in your own turnaround project. We wish you well on your journey to improve your school!

Introduction

Principal Ellen Morgan prepares for an exciting faculty meeting. She is looking forward to celebrating the school's positive direction with faculty. She has been principal of Henry Elementary School for three years, and during that time things have changed a lot. The school once had the lowest level of student achievement in the district. Parents avoided sending their children to Henry Elementary by asking for in-district transfers or by moving to other areas. Teacher morale was low, and student discipline referrals were high. The building itself, uninviting and dreary, reflected the school's atmosphere of negativity. There was no plan for success. By all accounts, Henry Elementary was a failing school.

In the three years since Principal Morgan took over leadership, student achievement has increased. The school now performs at the same or higher levels as schools in the top half of the district. Teachers are active members of collaborative teams, working together to solve problems and develop more opportunities for student success. An instructional leadership team guides the work, helping to establish school-improvement goals and providing teachers with professional development support. The custodial staff work hard to maintain a high level of cleanliness inside and outside the building. Members of an active parent-teacher group work together to increase parent involvement and promote positive aspects of Henry Elementary in the community.

While there are still issues to address, Henry Elementary is moving in the right direction on its path to success.

Principal Morgan's success in leading fundamental changes at Henry Elementary may seem too good to be true. The timeline, three years, may seem too short and the changes too vast, but successful school turnaround—making fundamental changes that take a school from failure to success—can be accomplished in a relatively short period of time with the right leadership. The right leadership includes the school principal, a representative leadership team, and developing a collaborative culture with everyone at the school. Although every school-turnaround situation is unique, there are common elements that should be the foundation of all turnaround efforts. We will explore these common elements and the strategies they entail within a model for school turnaround based on research and our own experiences turning around failing schools and working with leaders through the transformation process. We will show you how to lead a turnaround. We will show you how to *flip* your school.

What It Means to Flip a Failing School

It is the job of schools and educators to ensure that students advance their learning and meet specific benchmarks along the way. This is no simple task, and schools everywhere face heavy scrutiny at the district, state, provincial, and national levels, where student learning is measured and achievement compared. When schools are not meeting the primary goal of helping students to learn and grow, they could be in need of improvement. When there are serious deficiencies in student learning, they could be labeled as *failing* and in need of turnaround.

Let's look a little deeper into the concept of *failing schools*. According to Rosemary Papa and Fenwick W. English (2011), there is little mystery in identifying a failing school:

> Underperforming or failing schools are not hard to identify. A simple question to parents, community leaders, and students reveals that there is no issue in recognizing which schools are performing and which are not. The evidence is all around and is not confined to merely test scores published in the local paper or listening to real estate agents extol why property values in one area of the school district are high and others are much lower. (p. 1)

The term *failing school* seems to be the result of federal and state programs that seek to make improvements that guarantee success for all students. Coby V. Meyers and Joseph Murphy (2007) note that the term surfaced in the 1990s with the rise of the accountability movement, which linked student failure to school failure.

When large numbers of students fail to make anticipated academic gains or when smaller, disaggregated groups of students fail academically (such as those from specific subgroups such as students of color, students from lower socioeconomic groups, immigrant students, and so on), a school may be designated as "failing." Normally, the low performance of groups of students on a regional, state, or national test will be used to assign the failing designation.

A failing school is a school that performs significantly below expectations in meeting student needs, academically, socially, or emotionally. The degree to which a school is failing can be measured by standardized test scores, graduation rates, the quality of the learning climate, attendance rates (both student and faculty), student mobility, and a variety of other factors, or a combination of factors.

Lack of academic progress can have a variety of potential causes. Before beginning the turnaround process, school leaders must understand what may be contributing to poor academic performance as it affects the scope of the work ahead. Major issues with achievement could have several indicators, necessitating a comprehensive flipping or turnaround process. If a school is underperforming and not serving all students effectively, a turnaround plan addressing the entire school might be necessary. Alternatively, academic progress might be declining in just a few of the indicators, which requires less comprehensive turnaround work. For example, a school that is severely underperforming in a small number of academic areas, with a specific subgroup or subgroups at the school, or failing to show student growth or gains, might require a slightly different plan to successfully turn around.

We use the term *flipping* to describe the process of completely changing a school, so that students can be successful. This term people use often to describe the process of purchasing real estate in need of improvement, remodeling it, and then selling the much-improved property for a higher price, helps convey the totality of the work of school turnaround. The process of flipping fundamentally changes the real estate into something new, renewed, and desirable. Changes during the house-flipping process include major core changes (such as fixing the foundation and other structural elements) and more surface-level, cosmetic changes (such as adding fresh paint and new carpeting).

Flipping a school requires a high level of motivation, energy, and follow-through for a transformation to occur. With the help of a strong leadership team, a good leader can transform a failing school. By addressing fundamental elements inside the school, and coupling them with smaller, less complex changes, a good leader and leadership team can flip the school around—its course, how it is perceived, and its ultimate success as measured by student achievement growth. In our experiences working in schools undergoing turnaround, we have found that concentrating on two areas—implementing core structural changes along with addressing more visible changes—is the ideal focus for effective turnaround.

In the following section, we describe some specific types of improvement for school turnaround.

The Types of School Improvement for Turnaround

When flipping real estate, each property has different positives and negatives and requires a customized plan for improvement. The same is true for schools, and the school leader's first step is to determine what type of turnaround is needed. Meyers and Murphy (2007) identify five types of school improvement for turnaround projects. Let's take a look at the five types of school improvement and what each might entail.

School-Improvement Planning

School-improvement planning addresses necessary changes to the structure of the school's operation. For example, a school may have some of the following issues: the learning environment may not be well organized, faculty and student attendance may be a problem, teaching strategies may not match student learning needs, or the curriculum may not be relevant or well organized. In school-improvement planning, leaders simultaneously address several factors through a comprehensive school-improvement plan. In the real-estate world, this type of transformation might be thought of as a total remodel.

Expert Assistance

In this school-turnaround model, there may be areas that immediately stand out as to why the school's performance is below expectation. For example, student achievement in mathematics that is below state standards for a group or subgroup can point to a need to improve. In this improvement model, the school needs outside experts, such as consultants, district specialists, and retired school leaders to provide support to determine problem areas and interventions to get achievement back on track. In real estate, this type of change might be similar to when an interior decorator is brought in to make recommendations in a specific area of a property.

Provision of Supplemental Services

In some cases, a leader might turn around a failing school with supplemental services, such as providing viable transportation services to increase student attendance, conducting parental support programs, offering after-school tutoring for students who are behind academically, or hiring cultural liaisons to work with students and families from different cultural groups at the school. These services are meant to remediate an issue leading to the problem with student achievement, like poor student attendance. This type of school turnaround is like adding new features to or modernizing a portion of a property in real-estate flipping.

Adoption of a Reform Model

Some school-reform efforts are based on the implementation of an established, comprehensive school-improvement model. These models typically include multiple components designed to replace most or all of the components in a failing school. A school-reform model can be seen as an off-the-shelf solution to a failing school's problems. Typically, components of the reform model must match the needs of the failing school exactly and be implemented according to strict guidelines. Varying from the model may have a negative impact on results. In real estate, this might be akin to installing prefabricated components, such as new kitchen cupboards and new windows. They have to fit exactly within the existing structure or foundation of the school.

Reconstitution

Reconstitution means disbanding or dissolving the school and forming a new one. Sometimes faculty and staff are reassigned to other buildings, or they might be permitted to apply for positions in the reconstituted school. Reconstitution occurs when the existing staff may not be able to adapt to new practices or thought processes because previous frames of reference prevent them from considering new ways of working with students. There are variations of reconstitution. Some reconstitution processes replace just the leader or small groups of faculty such as a grade-level team or academic area, while others may replace more educators. The real-estate equivalent would be to tear down the existing structure and start over with a new design, new materials, and so on.

While all of the turnaround types are important and can address problems in unique situations, this book focuses on strategies and techniques to be successful with the first type of school turnaround: school-improvement planning. This type of school turnaround involves the principal and a leadership team working predominantly with the existing faculty and staff to flip the school.

How to Lead a School-Improvement Planning Effort

Leaders and instructional leadership teams tasked with implementing this specific school-turnaround model must develop a plan if implementation is to be successful. In this book, we share a model for school-improvement planning to help leaders successfully flip their schools. Figure I.1 outlines the step-by-step process that informs the model.

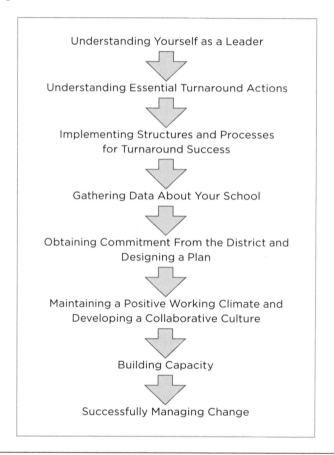

Understanding Yourself as a Leader

Understanding Essential Turnaround Actions

Implementing Structures and Processes for Turnaround Success

Gathering Data About Your School

Obtaining Commitment From the District and Designing a Plan

Maintaining a Positive Working Climate and Developing a Collaborative Culture

Building Capacity

Successfully Managing Change

Figure I.1: Step-by-step process for flipping your school with school-improvement planning.

Understanding Yourself as a Leader

Leading a failing school through turnaround is a challenging task. Leaders who seek to do so should know their leadership strengths and limitations, asking themselves, "How do I respond to conflict and chaos? When things seem to be falling apart around me, how do I react?" Successful turn-around leaders have the sense of calmness needed to endure challenging situations but the impatience to not become satisfied with the status quo.

Leaders must diagnose themselves as a beginning step in addressing the challenge they are about to tackle. Understanding their own abilities and ways of working and the scope of the external challenge is a critical component in determining what changes are possible and how they should be undertaken. Many leaders are optimistic by nature when it comes to analyzing situations. However, this attitude can be problematic when leading a failing school. A realistic analysis of the school's strengths and challenges is necessary to determine the goals and where to start with the turnaround effort. Consider the following as you design your initial approach:

- What are some of the capacities available within the school community?

- How can these capacities be used in addressing the issues at the school?

- What skills and capacities do I have to address the present situation?

- Is the school district ready and able to devote the resources (monetary, expertise, community support, and others) needed to provide a chance for success?

Can the difficult decisions you'll need to make be supported? Leaders must contemplate these and many other considerations before determining the right focus or the exact plan to begin to address the issues present in a failing school. If you think you might be lacking in some of the skills, you'll need to find a way to compensate. For example, if you feel uncomfortable in delivering the message that informs people of the problems and signals a need for a dramatic change, you'll need to find a way to increase your comfort. If you don't think you have the skill or experiences that will help you build a committed staff, you'll want to determine how you will build commitment with the help of the instructional leadership team. If you haven't thought through these needs, it could impede the success of your turnaround project.

Understanding Essential Turnaround Actions

The research related to school turnaround focuses on four essential turnaround actions common among schools. One of these essential actions is signaling a dramatic change. This action helps all in the school community know about the compelling reasons change is needed. This and the other three common actions found in the research will provide a foundation for the school-turnaround project.

Implementing Structures and Processes for Turnaround Success

You and your instructional leadership team should identify and implement structures to help the improvement plan be successful. Some of these structures include:

▸ Clear goals, strategies and activities, and outcomes

▸ Periodic celebrations

▸ Two-way communication strategies among the leader, the instructional leadership team, the staff, and the school stakeholders

▸ Follow-up and support processes

▸ Opportunities to monitor progress and make needed adjustments

▸ Ceremonies to remove practices no longer in use at the school

▸ Processes to reach agreement on and adopt common practices (such as behavior expectations, assessments and assessment strategies, and other common needs)

▸ Processes to encourage and use student voice in the turnaround effort

If you can develop the proper structures using some of these along with other strategies in this book to make turnaround changes part of the permanent structure or culture of the school, you will continue to have ongoing success flipping your school.

Gathering Data About Your School

Before beginning a turnaround process, leaders and leadership team members gather accurate data about their school. These data should include quantitative test scores and other standardized data, plus qualitative or descriptive data. Some data, such as poverty levels, the prevalence of poor teaching, the level of community involvement, the number and type of office referrals, and other possible contributing factors may only be accessible through conversations, observations, and other local assessment methods. Putting together related data from a variety of sources will help you and your leadership team get a good picture of what's happening overall in your school.

Obtaining Commitment From the District and Designing a Plan

Without the support of the school district, turning around a failing school can be very difficult or impossible. Turnaround leaders should work with the district to develop and refine a written plan that includes the goals, activities, resources, and outcomes of the turnaround project. Some changes may require additional funding while others may need a realignment of existing resources. Without a written plan, expectations can change and promises can be forgotten.

Effective leaders of school turnaround work with the instructional leadership team to develop both short-term and long-term improvement plans. These plans are focused, contain quick wins to build confidence, are easy to understand, have clear and measurable outcomes or deliverables, and include periodic opportunities to assess progress and make necessary changes. They also contain opportunities for staff to celebrate their efforts and accomplishments. Without recognition or celebration, school staff can lose momentum and fall back into old habits.

Maintaining a Positive Working Climate and Developing a Collaborative Culture

As the turnaround process unfolds, people can become tired and discouraged. It is important for the principal to work with the instructional leadership team to implement strategies that positively impact the climate of the school. Hard work can be fun, and staff should feel a sense of satisfaction, contributing to a culture of success. You and your instructional leadership team should also develop opportunities for and the skills to help people collaborate. Collaboration is based on familiarity and trust, so these are key elements to focus on in meetings. The climate and collaborative opportunities will help the school continue to develop in a positive direction.

Building Capacity

Leaders quickly realize that they can't turn a school around alone. They must develop leadership structures within the school that engage others in understanding the issues, developing plans, communicating these plans to their colleagues, and supporting them as they implement the plans. Your leadership efforts may begin with the development of a building instructional leadership team and eventually expand to include building capacity in the entire staff. Building leadership capacity in staff supports commitment to the initiative because people feel like a part of the improvement process rather than like the initiative is being *done to them*. By developing opportunities and skills for distributed leadership, the critical mass of support continues to motivate the turnaround process. Here are some examples of shared teacher leadership strategies that can help a school-turnaround effort.

▸ Developing an instructional leadership team to help facilitate communication and guide the turnaround process

▸ Using department chairs to help coach teachers on instructional improvement

▸ Forming collaborative teams who work together to examine student work, determine learning needs, and work with team members to implement new teaching strategies

▸ Using staffing allocations to provide representative teachers with release time to lead the teachers they support in understanding student achievement issues and help design plans to address them

▸ Encouraging teachers to schedule open visit times for other staff members to stop in their classroom, observe their teaching, and provide coaching and feedback

▸ Asking collaborative groups to present a sample of what they are doing in order to improve the achievement of their students

These are just a few of the many ideas that you and your instructional leadership team can implement to encourage others to lead their peers and colleagues and to help the turnaround effort be successful.

Successfully Managing Change

Even the most successful school-turnaround journeys encounter bumps along the way; things will not always go as planned, and unanticipated challenges will arise. It's important to carefully monitor implementation and address ongoing small but critical problems that you and your instructional leadership team find along the way. Sometimes, it's not the turnaround project that causes the problem, it is people's reaction to change that takes projects off track. Successfully managing change and people's needs during change is crucial for success.

Each chapter of this book covers one of these important elements of leading school turnaround.

Chapter 1, "Understanding Yourself as a Leader" provides an overview of research related to school turnaround. This research will help you as you evaluate your situation and begin your school-turnaround journey. Because each school is different and thus the turnaround process differs, it is important to match the processes and the strategies you implement with your school's unique needs.

Chapter 2, "Understanding Essential Turnaround Actions," explores techniques successful turnaround leaders use to build on their turnaround foundation and move the school along a path of continued success.

Chapter 3, "Implementing Structures and Processes for Turnaround Success," explores more foundational structures and processes that are needed to turn around student learning and achievement. Strategies in the chapter include those to meet schoolwide- and classroom-management needs, techniques to distribute or build leadership capacity with the staff, ways to develop structures to help students improve their learning, and working with teachers to improve their instructional strategies. All of these strategies help to address learning concerns and get a school back on the path to success.

Chapter 4, "Assessing and Developing Your Leadership Skills," focuses on several foundational aspects of school turnaround relating to leadership. It examines the leadership competencies needed for turnaround and provides opportunities for self-assessment and reflection along with strategies to effectively lead a turnaround effort.

Chapter 5, "Gathering Data About Your School," addresses how to move forward in gathering and analyzing important data to identify problems that are causing your school to fail.

Chapter 6, "Obtaining Commitment From the District," explores how to match school needs with support from the school district to make the school-turnaround process a success.

Chapter 7, "Maintaining a Positive and Productive Culture," examines the concept of school culture and how it can affect the success of your turnaround effort. This chapter also explores ways to enhance school culture during the turnaround process.

Chapter 8, "Building Capacity," provides practical strategies for building leadership capacity among staff and within instructional leadership teams to maximize your success as a turnaround leader.

Chapter 9, "Successfully Managing Change," provides ideas and strategies to successfully address needs during change and manage transition periods as you work to improve your school.

Throughout this book, we provide questions at the end of chapters to assist you in reflecting on the content.

Where to Begin

While flipping or turning around a school can be a complex undertaking, it is also very rewarding. It is gratifying to see staff and students filled with pride and confidence when they have successfully worked collaboratively to flip their school. Using the techniques you learn in this book will help you attain this outcome and accomplish success!

In chapter 1, "Understanding Yourself as a Leader," you'll begin the journey toward school turnaround. As you review the critical aspects of leadership needed for successful school turnaround, take a look at yourself to identify both the assets you bring and the areas in which you'd like to grow as a leader. This critical assessment will ensure you have the foundational leadership skills to successfully navigate the school-turnaround journey and make a difference in the lives of the students and staff at your school.

Chapter 1
Understanding Yourself as a Leader

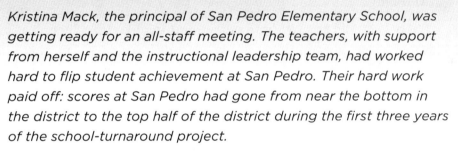

Kristina Mack, the principal of San Pedro Elementary School, was getting ready for an all-staff meeting. The teachers, with support from herself and the instructional leadership team, had worked hard to flip student achievement at San Pedro. Their hard work paid off: scores at San Pedro had gone from near the bottom in the district to the top half of the district during the first three years of the school-turnaround project.

To highlight this work and celebrate success, the instructional leadership team developed a fun ten-minute video of San Pedro featuring scenes of staff members and students as they worked and played. The staff enjoyed seeing the positive aspects of their school featured in the video.

After showing the video, Principal Mack told the staff how much she appreciated their hard work and dedication. She shared examples of the positive collaboration efforts witnessed, and then opened up the meeting for the staff to do the same. Their sharing of examples lasted more than ten minutes. In addition to sharing examples, several staff members said they planned to show the video to their students and congratulate them for their hard work in improving their achievement.

Principal Mack then drew names for door prizes donated by the parent organization and community partners. She ended the meeting with a school cheer designed by the instructional leadership team and the teaching staff. It was a very positive day at San Pedro!

Principal Mack had worked hard to build a positive and productive climate at San Pedro. She understood the role of emotion in building a culture of success. In this first chapter, you'll learn about an important foundational element in flipping a school—the emotional factors. It's easy to focus on mechanical issues like analyzing assessment results, developing school-improvement plans, and implementing interventions, but the emotional aspects can make or break the effort.

In this chapter, we discuss the importance of building a productive mindset in the school community and leadership attributes that support school-turnaround.

There is an old saying that goes something like this: "People don't care how much you know until they know how much you care." During the school-turnaround process, you have to show people you care about them in order to guide them on the journey. Without a caring and engaging atmosphere, any changes you make will be short-lived.

The Importance of Mindset

Author Carol Dweck (2007) in her book *Mindset: The New Psychology of Success* discusses this important aspect of success. In our own experiences, we have found that when leaders build a positive, can-do mindset in the staff, they open the doors to success.

In the scenario we shared at the beginning of the chapter, we see that Principal Mack understands this principle of mindset. She leads the school by being positive and having a can-do mindset herself. That positive mindset is contagious. The staff meeting is just one of the positive things she does to help reinforce a can-do mindset at her school.

In various staff and collaborative team meetings, Principal Mack talks about the importance of mindset in the success of San Pedro. She has the instructional leadership team read Dweck's (2007) book as a book study and then share the concepts with their other team members. She models a positive mindset when she is walking the halls of the school, interacting with students, staff, and parents, and in her communications.

Principal Mack also uses visual reminders of mindset at San Pedro. There are many signs and posters around the school that convey the message of positive thinking, setting and achieving goals, and the power of working together. The staff and students are immersed in the positive mindset of the school. It is a powerful influence in the success of the turnaround project at San Pedro.

In order for Principal Mack to lead the school and reinforce this productive mindset, she needs to take care of her own emotions and mindset. If she can't have a positive mindset and stay focused during the ups and downs of flipping the school, the rest of the staff and students will feel the impact of her struggles. Consider this: When traveling in an airplane, you usually hear the following safety announcement in relation to the oxygen masks that will drop down from the panel above, "Put the mask on yourself first before assisting others." This example reinforces the importance of self-care. If we don't monitor and take care of our own emotions, it's impossible to provide support for others. This self-care is vital in school-turnaround efforts.

Leadership Attributes That Support School Turnaround

In addition to this self-care, turnaround leaders should possess certain attributes including being enthusiastic and having a sense of adventure; being genuine, honest, and authentic; being a visionary; distributing leadership and developing others; empowering and trusting others; having grit and a can-do attitude; supporting a positive school climate that leads to a productive school culture; being knowledgeable about how to improve the quality of instruction; and being communicative and analytical.

Being Enthusiastic and Having a Sense of Adventure

If leaders aren't excited about their work, those they lead pick up on it right away. As school leaders, we need to be enthusiastic about taking on the challenge of flipping a school. We'll need to reframe our perspective to look at the transformation effort as an opportunity rather than as another task in a long list of responsibilities. This ability to "turn lemons into lemonade" is crucial. Let's see how Rafael Moreno does this in the following scenario.

> *Rafael Moreno is the principal of Hillside School, a preK–12 school in a rural area. The students have many learning challenges, but Principal Moreno has made it his mission to help them be successful. While he is driving to the school, he thinks about the challenges and what he might face each day. One thing that has helped Principal Moreno keep a positive mindset and enthusiasm for the work at hand is to change his thinking from "I have to deal with . . . ." to "I get to . . ." when considering his daily tasks. This process helps Principal Moreno keep his attitude positive and his enthusiasm high to keep leading the school-turnaround effort.*

Using such a simple reframing strategy may sound too good to be true, but positive self-talk can go a long way in helping us turn around negative thinking to keep ourselves motivated. There are some weeks where Principal Moreno has to use this strategy every day to keep his focus positive and retain his enthusiasm about the work.

Leading school turnaround is not for the fainthearted. Having a sense of adventure about the journey helps leaders maintain focus and a positive attitude during the ups and downs of the flipping process. Approaching turnaround as a leadership opportunity and thinking about it through a lens of excitement will help you maintain your focus as you continue to implement the school-turnaround process.

Being Genuine, Honest, and Authentic

Other elements essential to leading school turnaround are being genuine, honest, and authentic. When you are genuine, you are transparent and open. This is important in school turnaround because staff need to count on you to have a clear perspective. When you are genuine, people see that you practice what you preach and have integrity. When you reach out to them with empathy, they will know you mean what you say. When you compliment them, they will know what you say is true. When you praise them, they will know your words are accurate and not exaggerated. Being genuine also means telling the truth, whether the news is good or bad.

Honesty is related to being genuine. If you are honest, staff will know that you speak the truth, whether the news is good or bad. Honest leaders build a productive school culture because they foster accurate two-way communication. You provide your assessment of their efforts, teachers continue to improve, and you praise them when they do a good job.

The concept of being authentic—being real—is closely related to being genuine and honest. When a school leader is real, people can get to know him or her and can count on the leader to be open and honest. Authentic leaders share feedback in a diplomatic way but don't sugar coat messages. They look at the realities their school is facing, but they also focus on solutions rather than the problems. They are able to realistically evaluate a situation and calculate the chances of success. They set high but attainable goals for themselves and the school.

Being a Visionary

To effectively lead school-turnaround efforts, it's important to have a sense of vision and be able to articulate the vision to everyone in the school community. This vision should go beyond just words to evoke the emotions of the school community. Visionary leaders see past what is currently there to see what can be, and they have the ability to help others see the vision and become committed to its success.

Being a visionary also means being entrepreneurial and embracing innovation. School-turnaround leaders need to build on the ownership they instill in others and view their role as entrepreneurs. When leaders take personal responsibility for the success of the school as if it were a business, they change the dynamics. Entrepreneurial thinking helps leaders try new things and innovate in order to make their school a school of choice rather than simply the school students are assigned to attend. Innovation requires principals to think differently and look at new ways of doing things rather than just what's always been done. Consider the following scenario.

> Maya Ross, principal of Lincoln Middle School, determined that she should examine the way students receive extra help in their academic areas. In the past, there was a block of time in each school day where the students all went back to their homeroom and their homeroom teacher tried to assist with mathematics, language arts, science, and all of the other subjects. This structure was not working for students, and teachers expressed their discomfort in having to help students in academic areas where they may not have a mastery of the content.
>
> Principal Ross worked with the instructional leadership team to redesign the assistance program. Instead of going back to their homeroom for extra help, students went back to teachers in the academic area in which they needed help. This was more successful since students worked with teachers who had the content expertise to answer their questions. The process became so positive that even students who were not experiencing academic difficulty began going to see content-area teachers for enrichment and extension opportunities. Both students and teachers were much happier with the new process.

If Principal Ross and the instructional leadership team hadn't been able to be visionary and think outside of the box, they would never have implemented this successful new process.

A visionary leader is also inspirational. Leaders can inspire people through their actions and words and by exhibiting the attributes we discuss in this chapter. If you are honest and have integrity, your words of inspiration will be meaningful and your actions a model for the school community.

When leading a turnaround effort, principals and other school leaders are in the spotlight; people are watching you, how you interact with others, how you react to bad news or adversity, and how you handle yourself on a day-to-day basis. When you are sincere, real, and reflective, people get a sense of calmness and stability. This inspires them because they know you'll provide support and encouragement.

Distributing Leadership and Developing Others

For school turnaround to be successful, the principal needs to build ownership by sharing leadership. Once staff members feel they are an integral part of the change, they own it. When staff feel as though they have a stake in the school's destiny, they will invest much more in turnaround efforts than if they perceive themselves simply as employees. This happens when school leaders give others the opportunity to guide the work and be responsible for their own progress and success.

One role of a great leader is to help those around him or her grow and develop their skills. There are a variety of ways school leaders can develop others, including providing professional development, offering structures to promote collaboration and working together, building highly effective collaborative groups, providing professional feedback and coaching, and many other strategies. We discuss these strategies in depth later in the book. Developing others is a valuable skill for any leader, but it is especially important in school turnaround efforts in which new strategies and techniques are required to help students improve their learning and achievement.

Empowering and Trusting Others

Since we can't teach all of the students and improve their learning all by ourselves, we need to rely on others to help in the school-turnaround process. This takes a tremendous amount of trust on the part of a principal trying to flip a school. Because it is typical in leadership to have the view of "the buck stops here," some principals get nervous and micromanage their staff. When this happens, it can cause resentment on the part of those being micromanaged. According to Daniel Pink (2011) in *Drive*, a big motivator for followers is having some control over their work environment or some level of autonomy. When we empower others, we help them gain the capacities they need to be successful in the job, support them as they move forward, and trust them to do a good job.

Empowering and trusting do not mean we leave them alone. It is still important to provide support and follow-up to those we lead. We can do this by visiting classrooms, attending collaborative group meetings, talking with staff about challenges and victories, and doing many other strategies. If a staff member needs more support and guidance, leaders can provide those as well.

Having Grit and a Can-Do Attitude

In her book *Grit: The Power of Passion and Perseverance*, Angela Duckworth (2016) discusses the importance of determination and not giving up. Grit is important for leaders in general, and even more important for leaders of school-turnaround efforts. Flipping a school is a challenging process not likely to go smoothly. Having grit will help you persist even when it might be tempting to give up. Grit guides school leaders through the slower, more difficult aspects of the change process.

When a school is first identified as in need of turnaround, members of the school community can become very emotional and experience a sense of loss (we discuss this element in chapter 4). If you are the current principal when this happens, it's easy to take things personally. With the right kind of leadership, support, and guidance, most schools are able to turn around. It's important to model optimism in such a situation. If a leader gets discouraged, it's easy for teachers to also get discouraged. Optimism can be contagious. Approaching problems as opportunities changes the mindset of those you lead. It's important to pair your optimism with reality, however, so people know your positive thoughts are grounded in what is possible. You can be optimistic while also fairly considering potential issues or problems and seeking solutions.

Supporting a Positive School Climate That Leads to a Productive School Culture

School climate and culture are popular topics for discussion but they also spell success or failure for school-turnaround efforts. In the initial stages of flipping a school, there may be a negative culture resisting needed changes and supporting the status quo. You'll need to start by building relationships and collaborative structures in your school. A foundation for these relationships is to increase people's familiarity with each other by conducting activities at staff meetings, collaborative team meetings, and in other situations where people gather to help them learn more about each other. See how Janet Kwik, the principal at Able Middle School, uses an early fall faculty meeting to build relationships among the staff.

At the fall back-to-school faculty meeting, Principal Janet Kwik asked each staff member to bring an item or artifact that exemplifies something personal or professional about them. When staff enter the meeting room, Janet instructs them to grab a playing card and sit with others who have a matching card. At the beginning of the meeting, Janet shares her artifact with the rest of the staff. She goes around the room and asks each person to do the same. At the end of the meeting, she asks staff members to meet in their card groups and share what they learned about each other as a result of the activity. Faculty members share that they have learned a lot of things they never knew even after working together for a number of years. Janet informs the staff they would be using the new information they learned as they work together this upcoming school year.

In this example, we see how Principal Kwik implemented a strategy to begin to build a collaborative working climate. As the school year progresses, she will conduct more teambuilding activities to make the collaborative climate a more permanent way of operating in the school to form a strong basis for a collaborative culture.

Being Knowledgeable About How to Improve the Quality of Instruction

The quality of instruction has to improve for a school to turn around. A leader of a turnaround project needs to understand crucial or important aspects of instruction and how to customize them to fit the needs of the school. For example, in *Visible Learning*, John Hattie (2008), reports that holding discussions in classrooms has a positive impact on learning. Knowing this, you'll want to make your teachers aware of it, then determine how they'll implement more discussions in their classrooms. It may be that they need to improve the management of their class first in order to be able to hold more discussions. In other classrooms, teachers may need to help their students better understand some core concepts before engaging in discussions. In both cases, it is up to you to help teachers improve their instructional strategies and positively impact student learning.

Principals have many tools at their disposal to improve instruction, from helping teachers form collaborative teams that meet regularly to garnering the support of instructional coaches to assist teachers in implementing new strategies. Principals also have to have enough of an understanding of instruction to be able to determine if a teacher cannot learn and implement the needed instructional strategies for student success. In these cases, the principal may need to remediate, reassign, or not renew a teacher's contract. While these are unpleasant situations to have to deal with, they are necessary in order for the school to turn around and be successful. These types of actions draw on several of the strengths we identify in this chapter.

Being Communicative and Analytical

Leaders of successful school-turnaround projects are good at two-way communication: they communicate with stakeholders and seek to understand their ideas and perspectives on issues. In effective communication, clarity, accuracy, and tailoring the message to fit the needs of the audience are key elements to keep in mind.

Most of the attributes we talked about in this chapter have an emotional connection. The aspect of being analytical focuses on your ability to examine and make sense of data and information. Analysis is crucial in a turnaround project because you'll need objective, accurate, and meaningful data to understand what is happening in relation to student learning at your school. These data will also help you to assist in the development, implementation, and evaluation of the school-improvement plan. By being analytical, you'll be able to take a big-picture view of the school and help steer the ship toward success. We will be discussing the process of identifying and analyzing data later in this book.

Chapter Summary

Turning around a school can be a complex task. Whether or not a leader is successful can involve a variety of factors, but the foundation for success is in several key leadership attributes. In this chapter, we have provided a brief overview of some of these attributes. Not every leader must possess all of the attributes to the same degree, but knowing them will help you as you embark on your journey to turn your school around. Leading school-turnaround with these attributes helps to build a productive school culture that will empower everyone to success.

Another important part of flipping a school is understanding some of the background of the concept of school turnaround. In chapter 2, we provide a brief review of the major research and literature related to school turnaround as well as turnaround actions for leaders. This brief background will help you to think about the organization of your school-turnaround project.

Reflection Questions

As you reflect on the content of this chapter, answer the following questions.

---

1. Why is enthusiasm important when starting a school-turnaround effort? How can enthusiasm be spread to others in the school community?

---

2. How can principals inspire their staff members during a turnover project? Why is inspiration an important element to build while flipping a school?

---

3. Discuss the aspects of empowering and trusting others. How are these elements different than closely watching over others or micromanaging? What can supervising someone too closely cause to happen in their attitude and motivation for the job?

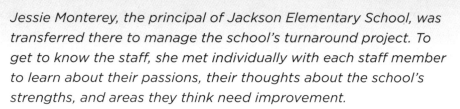

Chapter 2

Understanding Essential Turnaround Actions

Jessie Monterey, the principal of Jackson Elementary School, was transferred there to manage the school's turnaround project. To get to know the staff, she met individually with each staff member to learn about their passions, their thoughts about the school's strengths, and areas they think need improvement.

During these meetings, Principal Monterey shared the urgency for changing how teaching and learning are conducted at Jackson Elementary. She brought copies of the school-improvement plan with her to help clarify what would be flipped at the school. After sharing the urgency of the changes, Principal Monterey asked each staff member about his or her strengths, how he or she could contribute to the plan, and how she could assist each teacher in making changes. The meetings went extremely well; staff members indicated that they understood the need to change and believed they could contribute to the improvement effort. Principal Monterey noted staff ideas and planned to then share a compiled list of school strengths and necessary improvements.

In this scenario, Principal Monterey has taken the first steps in the school-turnaround process by signaling the need for drastic change, indicating what specifically would be changing, and how she planned to support each teacher in making those changes. In the previous chapter, we discussed some of the emotional aspects of school turnaround. In this chapter, we'll look beyond emotional characteristics and focus on observable behaviors from research that are common to leaders in school-turnaround efforts. Also in this chapter, we'll present a turnaround model based on a synthesis of the research for your use in managing the process.

Four Essential Turnaround Behaviors of Leaders

In the literature related to school turnaround, authors address common behaviors or steps that leaders take in implementing the school-turnaround process (Herman et al., 2008; Papa & English, 2011). These include signaling a dramatic change, consistently focusing on instruction, selecting quick wins, and building a committed staff.

Signaling a Dramatic Change

Signaling that a dramatic change needs to happen at a turnaround school is one of the first behaviors a leader needs to do after the school has been identified as failing. Leaders can communicate a major change by announcing it at a staff meeting, to departments, or to grade-level groups or content-level teams, or using some other small-group process. Leaders should also notify the school community of a dramatic change and why it needs to take place. Leaders can communicate the message through parent meetings, newsletters, the website, in blogs, or using whatever method will alert the most members of the school community. Communicating the need for dramatic change is important because it lets members of the staff and school community know changes are coming, and it helps them understand the rationale for the changes.

Some other examples of how and where school leaders can announce dramatic changes include the following.

> **Faculty meeting:** Be clear and direct about the reason and specific about the changes. For example, state, "As you know, our school has been identified as failing as a result of our latest state test scores. We need to make drastic changes in order to improve our student achievement. These changes include . . . ." Be sure to allow time for questions.

> **Newsletter:** Write an article about the roots of the problem and outline the upcoming changes and how these changes will address the issues.

> **Blog entry:** Write a blog entry on the school website to alert readers that the school has been identified as failing and that there will be major changes in the school. Remember to monitor the site if comments are enabled to answer any questions.

> **Letter:** Send letters to parents and other members of the school community letting them know about the need for drastic change at

the school and the reasons behind it. Invite them to contact you if they have any questions.

▸ **Parent and community meeting:** Holding a meeting is a great way to verbally let parents and community members know about the need for drastic change. Use visuals and handouts to help explain the details related to the changes.

Each message should address the informational needs of the group receiving it and consider how they take in and process information. Teachers may need more details about the change while community members without children in the school may be content with a more general message.

Signaling change provides clarity to members of the school community that things will be different. John Kotter (1996) calls this establishing a sense of urgency, or the rationale guiding the change. We find in our own school-turnaround experiences that developing a sense of urgency related to the future change not only works to cement collective understanding but helps to establish the buy-in needed to motivate teachers and staff to get focused for the change.

It's important to be clear and consistent when communicating about issues a school faces, but you don't have to do it with a negative tone. A colleague of ours took over leadership of a failing school. His communications to the school community clearly laid out major challenges, but also included details about the improvement plan and some of the benchmarks he would use to keep the school on track. Parents, teachers, students, and school district personnel clearly understood the problems and how he planned to lead the school to solve them. He didn't focus on what had gone wrong in the past, but on the path forward and on what each member of the school community could do to make the school effective in the future.

Let's see how Heather James, a middle school principal, communicates the need for drastic change in her first faculty meeting of the year.

> *Principal Heather James, the new leader of Prairie View Middle School, was transferred there to turn around the school, improve student achievement, and get teachers and staff working together in a more collaborative manner. Before the start of the school year, Principal James met with every staff member individually to get his or her impressions of the school. She used the information she gathered from these informal meetings as one data source to formulate her plan for the upcoming school year.*

> *She started the faculty meeting with an activity in which she had faculty and staff working together in randomly assigned groups to*

solve a problem. At the completion of the activity, she asked each team to present its solution to the assigned problem. Once teams finished presenting, Principal James addressed the group.

She said, "I've heard from quite a few of you that in the past you worked in isolation. Some of you even referred to our school as being like a series of independent teachers or silos. As you know, we have a lot of work to do in order to help increase our students' levels of achievement. Starting now, we will work together as a team, helping one another be successful and supporting one another just like we did in the activity today. No matter what, we will work together. This aspect of our school turnaround is non-negotiable and foundational to our success as a school."

During the remainder of the meeting, Principal James shared other dramatic changes that would occur at Prairie View. After each change, she asked staff to meet in small groups and discuss their perceptions and questions related to the proposed changes. By being clear and direct, Principal James communicated that the faculty would not be able to go back to their old ways. They would need to keep moving forward. Throughout the school year, whenever faculty started to fall back into their old ways of doing business, Principal James reminded them of the dramatic changes being implemented. Because she was clear about the dramatic changes at the beginning of the process, she could use these expectations to help keep staff moving in the right direction.

Consistently Focusing on Instruction

A second common behavior identified in the research (Herman et al., 2008; Papa & English, 2011) for turnaround leaders is to focus on instruction. While many factors influence success or failure, schools are measured by the learning and achievement of their students. Poor student achievement is not always caused by inadequate teaching. Socioeconomic factors, high student mobility, crime, and other home and community factors that schools can't control have a huge impact on student success in school. Effective instructional strategies matched to student learning needs can help overcome the impacts of some of these factors. In the book *Culturally Responsive Teaching and the Brain*, author Zaretta Hammond (2014) provides insight into brain-friendly instructional strategies that help students to move from being dependent to independent learners. In *Visible Learning for Teachers*, Hattie (2014) provides guidance to teachers and leaders for the instructional strategies that have the largest effect sizes in helping students learn.

School-turnaround leaders or leadership teams can select instructional strategies from these and other sources that have the greatest impact on student success.

It's not the purpose of this book to tell you which instructional strategies to use, but rather to encourage you to look at the needs of your students, then implement those strategies that best meet those needs.

Using an instructional leadership team to support grade-level or departmental collaborative teams is a highly effective way to examine learning needs and identify potential instructional strategies to address these needs. The leadership team can analyze assessment results, study course and academic offerings, study how time is spent in the school, assist grade-level or subject-area collaborative teams in developing student learning interventions, and complete a variety of other tasks. We usually call this team an *instructional leadership team*, but you can call them a school-improvement team, or whatever name you would like to give them. In the remainder of this book, we'll refer to the team working in concert with the principal to assist in flipping the school as the instructional leadership team. In chapter 3, we discuss the formation, roles, and other aspects of this type of team.

Let's see how Nathan Mason, a high school principal, uses his instructional leadership team to identify and support new strategies to focus on instruction in his school.

Principal Nathan Mason works with his instructional leadership team in his high school to identify three instructional strategies they want teachers to focus on during the fall semester. The first is to provide learning activities for students to do when they enter the classroom. The second is asking students to process information from the lesson in small groups (pairs, trios, and so on) at least three times during each lesson. The third involves using the exit card strategy to have students demonstrate what they have learned by answering questions on a card they must show the teacher in order to leave the classroom. The building instructional leadership team provides support and materials to departmental collaborative groups to implement during the fall semester.

For three months, these three instructional strategies are the focus of faculty professional development mini-sessions, monthly faculty meetings, and collaborative group meetings. The instructional leadership team shares articles related to these strategies for teachers to read and review. Instructional coaches at the school assist teachers as they implement the three strategies in their classrooms.

Throughout this period of intense focus, Principal Mason or an assistant principal do classroom walkthroughs, looking for evidence of implementation of the strategies. They provide specific feedback when they see a teacher using one of the strategies. They also ask teachers to bring examples of their implementation of the strategies to share and discuss at faculty meetings.

Teachers and collaborative teams are free to use other strategies as well, but everyone knows which strategies are the priority for teachers. During walkthroughs, Principal Mason and the assistant principals notice that students are more engaged in the lessons, there are fewer disruptions, and fewer students are sent to the office for discipline issues. Concentrating on a few strategies helps teachers to work together and collaborate, providing a sound learning environment for students. The common strategies establish consistency and a sense of predictability for students. Since there is consistency, teachers notice that other issues have been reduced, such as student tardiness and excessive absences. Some students tell their teachers they like to come to classes because they are more interesting.

Once teachers master the three strategies, Principal Mason works with the instructional leadership team to identify three new (but related) strategies to continue the clear focus on instruction. Since the teachers had success with the first set of strategies, they are confident and willing to add three new strategies to their classroom practices.

In Principal Mason's school, teachers know exactly what is expected of them and receive information and resources to help them successfully implement proven strategies. Principal Mason and the assistant principals positively reinforce teacher efforts to implement core teaching strategies. This common focus on instruction is an important factor in their school-turnaround effort.

Selecting Quick Wins

Leaders of effective school turnaround understand the importance of quick and easy victories. Visible and easy-to-secure changes can serve as tipping points that promote student success. Malcolm Gladwell (2002) defines a *tipping point* as "the moment of critical mass, the threshold, the boiling point" (p. 12). The tipping point can occur when enough energy is present to cause a change in the status quo. Gladwell (2002) contends that tipping points can spur huge changes in a situation, and he shares the story of the New York City police department in the early 1990s to illustrate how a tipping point can lead to bigger, substantive changes.

In the 1970s and 1980s, it was a common perception that crime was out of control in New York City. Several administrations tried to turn around the problem, only to fail; it seemed like an impossible problem to resolve. Then, in the early 1990s, the mayor and police commissioner developed a plan to build the perception that they were taking major steps to address the crime situation. Because New York is such a large city, they couldn't attack every issue contributing to the problem, so they picked several high-profile issues they could concentrate on and quickly turn around. Two of these areas were crime in the subway system and a lack of police visibility.

Before the new initiative, many crimes occurred on or near the subway: muggings, vandalism, people jumping the subway turnstiles to avoid paying subway fare, and so on. The initiative called for police to be highly visible inside and near the entrances of the subway system. Thus, arrests for offenses were swift, as was prosecution.

This focus on crime in and around the subway coupled with high police visibility dramatically reduced the crime rate in certain high traffic, high-visibility areas, giving the city the quick wins it needed to turn around public perception and build confidence in the turnaround plan, allowing the city to implement longer-term and more widespread crime reduction strategies. Getting the subway crime under control served as the tipping point; it let citizens know that New York City had the willingness and ability to tackle crime in an effective way.

Because New York City's crime problem was so big, large-scale turnaround took considerable time and required vast resources. Early in the process, city and police leaders needed to provide some highly-visible, quick wins to get things moving in the right direction. Once they attained enough of these quick wins, their effort reached a tipping point and the city was able to start addressing other problems. The quick wins in the high-visibility areas helped people think they were happening everywhere. The improved perception helped set the stage for a lower crime rate and the safer reputation New York City has maintained since the 1990s (Gladwell, 2002).

Victories show progress and help teachers and staff feel more comfortable and confident in implementing longer-term parts of the turnaround plan. Let's take a look at how Timberline Elementary Principal Lenny Carson selected visible, easy-to-secure improvements to achieve a tipping point in his turnaround effort.

*After determining the need for a school-turnaround effort,
Timberline Elementary Principal Lenny Carson works with
a leadership team of teachers to identify three major issues
connected to student achievement that are visible and offer
opportunities for quick wins: (1) the school building is poorly
maintained, (2) parents rarely stop in at the school—they simply
drop off their children, and (3) student absenteeism is high. In the
initial school-turnaround plan, these areas become the first areas of
focus for quick wins. The school-improvement plan includes longer-
term student achievement improvement goals, but those will take
more time to implement and bear results. In the meantime, Principal
Carson works with the custodial staff to make sure they thoroughly
clean the school, starts a program for parents to have free coffee
and conversation in the morning in the front entrance of the school,
and works with the staff to implement a follow-up communication
process where teachers call parents when students have missed
more than three days of school in a quarter.*

*Teachers and other staff start to notice the changes at the school,
the attitude of the students, and the improved comfort level of
some of the parents. Principal Carson ensures that his calendar is
clear during the morning drop-off period so that he is available to
talk with any parents who decide to stop in for coffee. As some
parents do stop by for coffee, he has informal conversations with
many of them. Several parents comment that in the past, they
only talked with the principal when their child was in some type of
trouble. Now, they are able to talk to him about positive topics too.*

*Parents who come in for coffee also make comments about the
cleanliness of the school. Principal Carson has instructed custodial
staff to keep the floors swept and to remove paper or debris once
students are in classrooms after morning entry. Soon, staff and
students notice less trash on the floors, and see students are more
likely to use the new brightly colored trash containers to help keep
the halls clean. Principal Carson periodically visits classrooms and
thanks students for their role in helping keep the school clean.*

*Finally, as a result of the follow-up communication with students
with excessive absences, fewer students are absent from school.
When Principal Carson asks a small focus group of students why
they miss school less often, they share answers such as, "I don't
want my teacher contacting my parents" or "I know that my*

teacher cares about me since she checks on me." It's clear that this strategy has created quick victories for Principal Carson and his school.

Principal Carson instituted three visible and easy-to-secure improvements at the start of his school-turnaround process that combined to provide a tipping point for even bigger school improvements. Because the building was cleaner and more organized, the school community began to have a more positive perception of the school as a good place for students. This helped to positively impact the school's learning environment. As more parents stopped in at the school for coffee and conversation, Principal Carson was able to begin building relationships. Teachers following up with absent students sent the message that teachers care about students and work together to support them. Because the staff were successful with these three strategies and saw quick results, they were more committed to making the more difficult changes needed to improve student achievement such as targeted interventions, a schoolwide behavior-management system, and implementing common assessments at the school.

In the preceding example, Principal Carson focused on noninstructional changes; however, quick wins can involve instructional elements as well. If an initiative is complex or has multiple parts, consider dividing it into small, attainable parts. Each portion of the larger implementation could be a quick win. Consider the following instructional and noninstructional projects that could provide quick wins for a school-turnaround effort.

▸ Implementing common schoolwide processes (such as visitor sign in, student announcements, messages for students, teacher requests for resources, and so on)

▸ Maximizing staff and administration visibility in potential problem areas (such as hallways, bus drop-off and pick-up areas, parent drop-off and pick-up areas, and other high-traffic and high-visibility areas)

▸ Eliminating bells and replacing them with music for a more pleasant passing time, fixing bottleneck areas where student walking traffic slows, and varying the times of events (such as lunch) to eliminate long lines and waiting

▸ Implementing common, schoolwide behavioral expectations (such as a signal for attention, proper voice levels in class, expectations for behavior during passing times, and other common expectations)

- Having all teachers implement the same procedures for assignment submission (such as using common assignment headings, common locations in classrooms for submitting assignments, and so on)

- Conducting home visits to show parents the school cares about children and families

- Examining the time on task in classrooms and implementing simple strategies to use more class time for instruction

- Improving student engagement during class

- Implementing processes to gather and use student voice in the school

- Focusing on techniques to improve computation in mathematics

- Making the front office area more welcoming

- Improving the landscaping by the exterior of the school building

Quick wins alone won't turn around a school, but they will build the confidence and enthusiasm needed to move forward with more complex changes. As we saw in the scenario with Principal Carson, the quick wins implemented at his school served as a foundation for adding more complex strategies later.

Building a Committed Staff

No school-turnaround process will be successful without a committed staff. As we mentioned in the introduction, sometimes an entire school is reconstituted, as leaders replace the staff with new teachers who are committed to the change process; however, most often, leaders have to work with an existing school staff, finding ways to motivate them and help them to be successful in the turnaround process. Building staff commitment, or buy-in, is important to the success of the turnaround effort, and, ultimately, to the school.

Jim Collins (2001) writes, when building a committed staff, it is critical for leaders to "get the right people on the bus." Collins also believes that we need to have people in the right seats and moving in the right direction. These points relate to building a committed staff.

This might require that leaders move some staff members to other schools or settings that better suit their strengths and level of commitment to the success of the school. Staff need to be in the right positions in the right locations to access and implement their skill sets most effectively. Moving one or two negative people to another school can send a message to staff that the improvement effort is serious, and so can moving positive or highly skilled and motivated people to positions of increased responsibility. Both changes enable staff to better concentrate on the success of the turnaround project. Eliminating negative influences can be a tipping point for success and so can increasing positive influences.

When transferring staff members to new positions or new teams, leaders should be prepared to share their rationale for the changes. In most cases, rationale is only necessary for those directly involved in the transfer. In cases involving positive moves, more people may be informed.

Providing reasons for staff changes lets people know the process has been well thought out rather than is something that has happened arbitrarily or for personal reasons. Staff may voice concerns about the changes in the short-term, but this will normally diminish once people are able to see the positive effects of the changes.

Having the right people in the right positions is one aspect of building a committed staff, but it alone isn't enough. Staff members need to learn the skills necessary to be successful in their roles. They may benefit from professional development or retraining to succeed in the turnaround setting. Aligning professional development and professional growth plans with the needs of the school will help staff build the necessary skills while also strengthening school-improvement efforts.

Building a committed staff for turnaround can be challenging. Leaders must find ways to motivate staff members, rather than merely giving them orders and directives. It takes a lot of work on the part of a turnaround principal to balance the use of *supportive leadership* and *directive leadership*. In supportive leadership, you do things to show people you care and that you support their work. You might cover a class so they can attend a family event or compliment them on their work. In directive leadership, a leader may be more authoritative, telling staff what needs to happen. This type of leadership may be helpful when you have to solve problems or keep people's efforts on track. Leaders will find that there are times when it is necessary to be directive with teachers and staff during the turnaround process, but autocratic methods should not be the default mode for leading groups through change. Leaders need to use supportive strategies to build commitment and move the school forward.

Neither supportive nor directive leadership practices are all bad or all good on their own. They can become problematic when used exclusively or to an excess.

In the following example, let's take a look at how a principal, Miguel Vasquez, worked to develop a committed staff for his school-turnaround project.

> Principal Miguel Vasquez is assigned to turn around James B. Madison Elementary. While conducting his preliminary assessments of the school, he notices that teachers and students do not seem very committed to the school. There is no school mascot, no school colors, and no school pride. The teachers and the students appear to be going through the motions of engagement without any real purpose or passion behind their activity. Principal Vasquez knows something needs to change.

> He meets with the school's instructional leadership team to discuss the issue. Together, they design a school mascot and school colors. Miguel suggests that they have a slogan—tiger pride—that they use to build student and teacher commitment to the school.

> Principal Vasquez buys the staff polo shirts in school colors featuring the Madison tiger, which they wear every Friday. In the front of the school, Principal Vasquez displays photos of every grade-level team in their tiger pride shirts. He starts every assembly with the words, "Tiger pride!" as a signal to get student attention. He even teaches staff members a pride cheer that they perform at every staff meeting.

> Principal Vasquez focuses on other strategies to build staff commitment as well. He provides support with actions, such as placing positive notes in staff mailboxes, leaving positive phone messages for staff, covering classes when teachers have appointments, and hosting regular celebrations of success.

> As his first year at Madison Elementary progresses, Principal Vasquez notices more and more commitment on the part of teachers. They are becoming more committed and caring about the school and the students. Most of the teachers are using the tiger pride signal to get the attention of the students in class, and most of the staff wear their school shirts on Friday. Teachers have started to collaborate and help each other when someone experiences a problem. In the mornings before school and after

school at the end of the day, he notices that a majority of the teachers are in the halls and other common areas of the school interacting with students.

Principal Vasquez used simple strategies to build staff commitment to the school. Once he established this initial foundation of support, he began working with the school's instructional leadership team to focus on teaching and learning strategies to move learning forward. The instructional leadership team used the good will they helped develop during the focus on school pride to now focus on instructional improvements. This reminded the teachers how successful the school pride effort was and told them they'd have the same support and experiences as they adopted and implemented new instructional strategies. The instructional leadership team scheduled fun and engaging learning events to help staff learn new instructional strategies. They included collaboration, sharing, and celebration in the processes similar to those used when they adopted the school mascot. They set the right emotional tone for the new instructional strategy support process to be successful. The tone and the fact that much of the improvement effort was being guided by a collaboration between the principal and the instructional leadership team helped staff to commit to or buy into the plan.

In leading the turnaround effort, both the instructional leadership team and Principal Vasquez had to constantly do things to keep their enthusiasm high and stay focused and positive. They did fun and energizing team-building activities at their meetings, discussed the positive changes they noticed at the school, and employed other strategies to charge their batteries and keep a positive mindset. They knew if they could remain positive, they could help their colleagues remain positive as they implemented the needed changes. They shared some of these strategies and ideas they used as a team when they worked with their colleagues to help build enthusiasm with them. Even though there were challenges and setbacks, the focus on the positive activities and conversations helped to keep everyone moving forward.

Building commitment is not always an easy task; not every staff member will jump on board and become committed to the improvement plan at the start of the process. The key is to build a critical mass of support. By critical mass we mean a majority supports something or the collective group energy supports it. Without a critical mass, initiatives have a hard time being successful. Building committed staff establishes a critical mass to be successful.

Since the four strategies we've discussed in this chapter are essential for school-turnaround success, we've provided a template for your use in developing them during your turnaround project. Figure 2.1 is a planning template to assist school leaders in implementing the four strategies. Visit **go.Solution Tree.com/schoolimprovement** for a free reproducible version of this figure.

Leadership Behavior for School Turnaround	Existing School Structures for Immediate Implementation	Plans or Strategies for Further Implementation
Signal a Dramatic Change		
Consistently Focus on Instruction		
Select Quick Wins		
Build a Committed Staff		

Source: Herman et al., 2008; Papa & English, 2011.

Figure 2.1: Planning improvement efforts using the four behaviors.

Visit **go.SolutionTree.com/schoolimprovement** for a free reproducible version of this figure.

Figure 2.2 shows an example of a completed template using the four recommendations.

In this section of the chapter, we have shared with you four leadership behaviors or strategies that researchers have found to be common in school-turnaround projects. These strategies serve as a foundation for successfully flipping or turning around a school. Without stating the need for a drastic change, the turnaround project lacks importance or immediacy. Unless the principal and the instructional leadership team are able to build a committed staff, the project will not have the synergy needed for success. If the school-turnaround project only focuses on cosmetic or surface changes and not on improving instruction, student learning and achievement will not be positively impacted.

The four leadership behaviors highlighted in this chapter provide a foundation upon which to build the school-improvement plan. In chapter 3, we will discuss essential structures and processes that need to be considered in flipping or turning around a school. These structures and processes focus on the heart of improving student achievement and improving the organization of the school and its learning culture.

Leadership Behavior for School Turnaround (Herman et al., 2008; Papa & English, 2011)	Existing School Structures for Immediate Implementation	Plans or Strategies for Further Implementation
Signal a Dramatic Change	• Student achievement data have been analyzed and the problem areas identified. • There is an instructional leadership team in place, and members know their role in assisting in school turnaround.	• Present student achievement data trends for the previous three years at a faculty meeting. • Share a written copy of the school-improvement plan at the faculty meeting. • Share the most important aspects of the school-improvement plan at the faculty meeting. • Conduct follow-up by meeting individually or in small groups with teachers to discuss the plan after the faculty meeting. • Ask the instructional leadership team members to check in with teachers they represent after the meeting to make sure everyone is following through on expectations.
Consistently Focus on Instruction	• The instructional leadership team has identified the problems in the present teaching strategies. • Instructional coaches are in place to assist teachers in learning new strategies. • The principal and coaches currently conduct walkthrough classroom visits.	• The instructional leadership team selects three strategies to focus on during the initial turnaround process. • Principals and coaches look for evidence of the three instructional strategies during classroom walkthroughs. • The principal and instructional leadership team ask teachers to bring to their collaborative team meeting examples of how they have implemented the three strategies in their classrooms. • The instructional leadership team asks collaborative teams to generate ways of using the three strategies in their classrooms. • Add a section to staff meetings to discuss instructional strategies.

Figure 2.2: Sample planning improvement efforts using the four behaviors.

continued →

Leadership Behavior for School Turnaround (Herman et al., 2008; Papa & English, 2011)	Existing School Structures for Immediate Implementation	Plans or Strategies for Further Implementation
Select Quick Wins	• Teaching strategies are already in place related to the new, needed strategies. Teachers can build on existing strategies to support the needed strategies.	• Ask teachers in which areas they think it would make the most sense to start improvement efforts. • Focus on student attendance, follow up with families, and implement one strategy to increase student engagement in the classroom. • Hold a celebration when student attendance has increased by 10 percent. • Hold a celebration when each teacher is using at least one new student-engagement activity each day.
Build a Committed Staff	• Involve committed staff members in initial implementation; ask them to talk to staff to help others become more committed.	• Tap informal leaders who are already committed to the school and have them mentor other teachers to increase their commitment. • Adopt school colors, a mascot, a school motto, and so on. • Hold special days when all faculty show their school spirit, such as by wearing their school colors. • Let teachers know you appreciate their work with positive face-to-face comments, notes, special events, and so on.

Chapter Summary

Earlier, we met Principal Ellen Morgan, who was getting ready to meet with teachers to celebrate their success with the school-improvement plan. Principal Morgan and her staff had transformed Henry Elementary from a failing school to one moving in the right direction. Let's check back to discover the results of their discussion from the staff meeting.

As Principal Morgan presents the list of positive changes that have occurred in her school as a result of school-improvement planning, she notices that staff members seem to be happy and have a lot of pride in the work they have done. Several smile and comment to one another as they listen to Principal Morgan highlight their list of accomplishments.

After her presentation, Principal Morgan opens up the meeting for teacher comments. One teacher, Len, indicates that he finds several strategies that teachers can implement within short time frames very effective. He says using these strategies motivated him and helped him feel that he could accomplish the rest of the goals. Several other teachers nod their heads in agreement with Len.

Another teacher, Charli, comments that she likes the way Principal Morgan lets the teachers know how much she appreciates their efforts. She especially likes the regular comments Principal Morgan shares with staff and the short celebrations she offers as a way of thanking teachers.

Finally, Myrna, one of the most senior upper-elementary teachers, sums it up by saying that Principal Morgan's support and encouragement helped her believe that she could be successful with their students, something she had not experienced with other principals in the past. She appreciates that Principal Morgan encourages her while also communicating high expectations for her teaching. This balance helped Myrna stay focused during the first year of the school-improvement plan. Again, many other teachers nod their heads in agreement.

Afterwards, Principal Morgan feels good about the meeting and the progress she helped staff make. She looks forward to their work together in the upcoming year.

Principal Morgan was able to celebrate the success of her school-improvement plan because she was able to work with her teachers and share or distribute the leadership, not against them. She used many of the strategies we discuss in this book to empower teachers to success rather than just telling them what to do. For example, she was out and about in the school on a daily basis interacting with and listening to teachers. This informal process enabled her to find out about issues before they became major problems. She also met individually with each teacher every semester to talk with him or her about what was going well and what needed her attention. These are just two strategies she used to open up communication and keep the turnaround effort moving forward.

This is not to say that Principal Morgan had success with every teacher; some teachers could not accept the fact that they needed to make changes or lacked the skill or motivation to make them. Because of the changes, some of these teachers became uncomfortable working at the school and decided to leave and work somewhere else. A couple of teachers had become members of factions that wanted to be negative and contribute to the chaos that was happening at the school. When the majority of the staff decided to move forward and make key changes, these negative people saw their power base of supporters erode. Some of them became uncomfortable and decided to change settings.

Principal Morgan wanted the school to be a happy and healthy community and a good place to work, but she knew some people may not be interested in moving in the new direction and would decide to leave. She tried to still support them and maintain a good, professional relationship. In general, she was able to nurture a supportive and collegial atmosphere at Henry Elementary School that enabled success for both teachers and students.

In this chapter, we examined key elements of school turnaround to help leaders understand the process, know what to focus on, determine needs, and take necessary steps in their turnaround efforts. In the next chapter, we explore leadership style and the strengths and limitations it brings to school-turnaround planning. You will learn practical strategies to help you understand how you lead and maximize your success as a school leader.

Reflection Questions

As you reflect on the content of this chapter, answer the following questions.

1. What are the key strategies and behaviors that school-turnaround leaders implement for success?

2. Why is it important to diagnose school needs and determine available resources before taking on a school-turnaround project?

3. How do you think you might be able to build commitment to the school and the turnaround process with your staff members?

4. What strategies and ideas did you find helpful in this chapter?

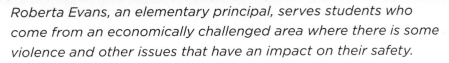

Chapter 3

Implementing Structures and Processes for Turnaround Success

Roberta Evans, an elementary principal, serves students who come from an economically challenged area where there is some violence and other issues that have an impact on their safety.

Principal Evans works with her teachers and staff to establish and maintain a structured, consistent, and safe atmosphere. In the first year of their turnaround project, the school organized extra learning opportunities for students after school. When students experience academic difficulties in the classroom, they are able to stay after school to try to improve their achievement. Teachers run the after-school sessions, helping students with multiple academic areas.

After operating this model for two years, Principal Evans and the faculty are frustrated that achievement hasn't improved as much as they would like. The same students seem to be getting low grades in their classes and scoring poorly on standardized tests. Teachers comment that working with these students is difficult, and students comment that the sessions are not very helpful and they don't like to attend. The teachers sometimes express frustration that they can't always help students with learning issues in areas outside of their expertise.

The instructional leadership team holds a series of meetings to gather information about the potential causes of the problem and try to address it to improve the program. After careful review, the team agrees that the current structure is problematic and learning challenges are best addressed as much as possible in the classroom by classroom teachers. In order for this to happen, teachers need new strategies, support, and a way to assess student challenges and a plan for how to address them.

The instructional leadership team decides the school should implement response to intervention (RTI), where teachers work together to implement a three-tiered approach to learning. In year one, teachers work together to refine their curriculum so it has a more clear focus on the academic standards and generate learning strategies to help all or most students become successful on their first learning attempt. Students who do not learn on the first attempt receive extended learning opportunities in the second tier to be successful. A third tier also exists for the small number of students who need extended help for longer periods of time to reach learning goals.

The idea of using a new approach that has been tested in other schools is motivating to the staff. They are ready to start implementing the first stages of the program soon.

This example shows the importance of building a good foundation for turnaround by implementing proven strategies and processes to improve student achievement. Principal Evans built trust with the teachers in her school by using the care factor and by working closely with the instructional leadership team to study and analyze data, make decisions, and implement strategies for systemic change. Without care and leadership, Principal Evans and the team would not have been able to successfully implement a system for addressing student needs at the foundational level. Instead, their work might have culminated in another disruptive program imposed on staff by the principal, one meant to be successful but that didn't work.

In this chapter, we share more specific strategies, structures, practices, and programs that are essential to flip a school. We'll focus on two areas: (1) strategies to use with students and (2) strategies to use with staff. These structures include a schoolwide behavior-management plan, structures for giving students a voice, ways to distribute leadership, structures to increase success, structures to improve instruction, and ways to make rituals, ceremonies, and celebrations a priority.

Implementing Schoolwide Behavior Management

Establishing and following through with a schoolwide behavior-management plan is an essential part of flipping a school. Entire books have been written about this topic, so the brief description we provide here is not designed to give you all the tools you need to master this crucial aspect of school turnaround. Instead, we provide several essential aspects of schoolwide behavior management for your consideration.

Schoolwide behavior management strengthens the foundation of your school-turnaround effort. If chaos and disorganization are the norm at your school, you will make little progress in the area of instructional improvement. Unless the learning environment is stable and predictable, students won't have the atmosphere they need for success.

There are many off-the-shelf behavior-management programs you can choose, or you can create your own. In our book *Thriving as a New Teacher* (Eller & Eller, 2016), we provide ideas and strategies for use in both classrooms and common areas of the school. These ideas are based on making behavior management a learning activity for students and matching the behavior-management expectations and procedures to the school climate you want to reinforce. The success of this behavior-management process is based on everyone in the school having common expectations and teaching and practicing the desired behavior skills in an attempt to reinforce them to become good habits for students.

We suggest addressing two areas in your behavior-management plan—(1) management of common areas and (2) management of classroom procedures—and developing expectations for student behavior within both of these areas. Some examples of specific areas of behavior management in each area follow.

1. Management of common areas
   - Expectations for behavior during movement within and around the school
   - Expectations for behavior during group meetings and assemblies
   - Expectations for behavior when entering and leaving the school
   - Expectations for behavior when taking care of personal needs (visiting lockers, taking restroom breaks, and so on)
   - Expectations for using technology (cell phones, personal devices, and so on)

2. Management of classroom procedures
   - Expectations for assignment completion
   - Expectations for submitting completed work
   - Expectations for voice levels during activities
   - Expectations for being on time for class

These lists are just a start; there are many possible expectations to manage within a school building. All staff members should share and reinforce schoolwide expectations. These expectations should also be stated positively. Some schools state the expectations by naming all of the expected behaviors, while others state them in a more general sense describing combined student actions based on multiple expectations. For example, a general expectation statement might be, "Students will be respectful." A specific behavioral expectation statement might sound like, "Students need to pass in the halls in an orderly manner." Both of these methods of stating expectations can be effective if students and faculty have a clear understanding of what is expected of them.

Figure 3.1 shows a list of expectations that contains both general and specific statements.

LONGVIEW PANTHERS
Schoolwide and Classroom Expectations

PRIDE *for Self*
Bring all materials to class.
Be working when the bell rings.
Put forth your best effort.

PRIDE *for Others*
Use respectful language, actions, and gestures.
Demonstrate active listening.
Maintain physical space.

PRIDE *for Property*
Use materials with care and respect.
Keep the environment clean.
Leave all property as you found it or better.

PREPARED, RESPECT, INTEGRITY, DEPENDABILITY, EFFORT

Figure 3.1: Sample schoolwide expectations.

The list in figure 3.1 addresses almost any issue that could arise in a school. It is clear and easy to understand for students and easy for staff to reinforce. At the school in the example (figure 3.1), the staff members each explain the expectations in small groups in their classrooms. They also provide an opportunity for students to learn the skills by practicing the desired behaviors.

Giving Students a Voice

Student voice is a key element for success in school turnaround. Since students are members of the school community that is being improved, they should have a voice in some of the processes that impact them the most. Schools can start a Student Voice Council or Student Committee for students to share their feedback and opinions about those school policies and practices that impact them. Some areas where student voice is helpful include:

- Making changes to processes such as passing time between class, problems with bottleneck areas in the school, and other common area issues that impact students

- Helping to set up periodic celebrations for improvement, such as reduced tardies, improved attendance, and so on

- Providing student perspectives on certain policies such as technology use, dress code, cell phone policies, and so on

- Finding out student perceptions related to recently implemented turnaround strategies such as learning interventions, after-school programs, student mentoring programs, and other related areas

These and other involvement opportunities help to give students a voice during school turnaround and set a positive tone in the school. Leaders and staff find ways to get the students involved in the process of behavior management. This can happen through having students participate in determining classroom policies and procedures, asking student government (student council) groups to help set the behavior expectations, or employing a wide variety of other strategies. We won't discuss this aspect in this book, but will focus on other unique ways students can be more involved in their own behavior management.

If students are involved in some aspect of determining their environment, they will be more committed to and interested in its success. If students feel that the staff care about them and their welfare, they are more likely to become meaningful partners in the turnaround process.

A team approach to behavior management involving students is an idea called a reflection council. The reflection council strategy is meant to build student confidence and strengthen relationships between teachers and the students. The process works like this.

1. The teacher handwrites a letter to the student about a concern (attendance, behavior, attitude, and so on). The handwritten letter helps to make the process more personal for the student.

2. The teacher gives the letter to the student.

3. The teacher shares the letter with the reflection council (members include the student's principal or dean—assistant principal, counselor, or some other student advocate—the teacher completing the invitation letter, the school psychologist, a special education teacher, and a school intervention teacher).

4. The reflection council schedules a meeting with the student.

5. At the meeting, the refection council meets with the student, reads the letter, and asks the student to share his or her perspective on the issue.

6. The reflection council helps the student develop a plan to address the concern the teacher has expressed.

7. The reflection council follows up later with the student to ensure the plan is successful.

The members of the reflection council need to focus on listening during the process and understanding the situation. They also need to be able to ask the student open-ended questions to help him or her process the situation and develop some possible solutions. The reflection council process helps to put the solution for the problem or situation in the student's hands. It also helps teachers develop an understanding of the issues causing the problem.

This strategy promotes the care factor and promotes positive school culture because the council is not designed to be punitive. Instead, it is designed to show each student how much he or she is cared for and assist students in developing positive problem-solving strategies to deal with challenging behaviors.

Figure 3.2 shows a sample memo describing the reflection council to staff members. Figure 3.3 (page 48) shows a copy of a sample student letter read at the beginning of each reflection council meeting.

Distributing the Leadership

Giving staff members opportunities to take on leadership responsibilities allows them to grow, develop their skills, and build a deeper commitment to the success of the school. Earlier in the book, we shared information about the importance of promoting buy-in and engagement for successful school turnaround. To go even further than buy-in, we recommend leaders embrace Kouzes and Posner's (2017) ideas about the importance of making members of an organization feel like owners. When employees are owners, they have an increased level of commitment and take the success of the organization seriously. A good way to build teachers' level of ownership of the turnaround effort is through distributing leadership by dividing staff into leadership teams.

The Reflection Council Process at Smith Middle School

Overview

In one month, we will introduce a new problem-solving process at Smith Middle School. This process is called the reflection council. The reflection council will help students who have a pattern of misbehaviors develop and follow through on plans to improve their behaviors and get back on track.

This memo provides information about the procedures for the reflection council so staff members can understand and use this process.

General Reflection Council Information

- Members of the reflection team: Student's dean, teacher completing the invitation letter, school psychologist, special education teacher, school intervention teacher

- Reflection council meeting day and time: Thursdays after school from 3–4 p.m.

- Duration of each reflection council meeting: Meet with three students in twenty-minute increments

- Meeting location: Room 002 (small room)

Student Selection for Reflection Council

- Students may be selected who have multiple in-school suspensions, poor attendance, poor assignment completion, twelve or more unexcused absences from school, or other consistent behavioral issues.

Procedure

1. The dean of students, principal, or teacher will call the parents and notify the student about the reflection council and invite the parents to be a part of the meeting.

2. Involved staff members will be invited to write a letter to a student sharing their concerns about an issue or behavior. The letter will also be shared with the reflection council.

3. The student and staff member or teacher is invited to an upcoming reflection council meeting.

4. The staff member introduces the student and gives the student the letter describing the concerns.

5. When the student is ready to talk, he or she indicates this to the panel.

6. Much like interviews, the panel will take turns asking questions; one staff member will take notes during the conversation.

7. The last ten minutes are reserved for the student to use if he or she has any questions.

8. The panel will tell the student that they will review the notes and agree on next steps, and the student's dean will communicate the next steps the following day.

9. If a student makes it back to the panel a second time, parents will need to be present.

Precursors to Council Implementation

- Train panel on restorative justice conversations.

- Explicitly communicate to all students what the panel is and how the school is going to use it.

Figure 3.2: Sample memo describing the reflection council process.

Dear (student name),

The first thing you need to know is that we care about you more than you know. We believe in you. We want to be here with you today because we know you can do this, and you will show us how awesome you are.

We come into this meeting with a mindset that everyone makes mistakes. There is always a reason or outside factors that play into everyone's actions.

We also know that this is not going to be easy for you, and that's okay. Sometimes, we all have to do things in life that are not easy, but we grow from those experiences. We want you to grow from this experience, and we will support you throughout this conversation.

Some tips for you to make this a good experience and one that we can all learn from are:

1. *Be honest*—We want to know your truth. This is your space to share with us your perspective. We value your thoughts and words.

2. *Be humble*—Admit to your wrongdoings and try to problem solve with us. You need to take responsibility for your actions, and that is a very brave thing to do. We know it's a hard thing to do. We are here to support you.

3. *Be reflective*—Think about your feelings and the feelings of everyone else involved. Showing empathy shows us that you are willing to make amends to your actions.

Again, we care about you which is why we are here. When you are ready, let us know and we will get started.

The Reflection Council wants you to be successful in making changes here in your school. We will follow up with you in about two weeks to see how things are going and to provide you with support to keep things on track.

Sincerely,

The Reflection Council

Figure 3.3: Sample student letter for reflection council meeting.

Distributed leadership is a process where the school leader shares or gets others involved in aspects of leading a school. The process may include strategies for those involved in sharing the leadership to learn important information, have opportunities to process and analyze this information, and be involved in making decisions that involve policies or processes that impact their school.

By sharing or distributing leadership, the school principal gets people involved in guiding the school-turnaround project. Leaders can provide distributed leadership opportunities through the use of an instructional leadership team, a leadership cabinet (a group advising the leader), collaborative teams, or a variety of other techniques. A key aspect of distributed leadership is sharing leadership at the appropriate level.

The types of leadership teams you implement during turnaround will vary based on the structure, strengths, and limitations of your school. Your leadership style and the type of turnaround process you are implementing will also play a role. The role of each individual within each team may vary as well, depending on the school. In some cases, the instructional leadership team might have a significant role while in other cases, the team might only provide input for the leader to consider or act as a liaison between the principal and the staff. In the following sections we describe several types of teams leaders can use to distribute leadership.

Instructional Leadership Teams

The most important team structure in a school that is involved in the turnaround process is the instructional leadership team. Members of instructional leadership teams represent and speak for the rest of the staff and provide the staff with information and ideas to help them move into new and better ways of doing things. Team members may gather information from and share information with those they represent, gather and analyze data to assist in the development of the school-improvement plan, provide guidance to teachers in implementing strategies and activities, assist in measuring results, make necessary adjustments to help keep the plan on track, schedule periodic celebrations, and do other important tasks. In addition to these tasks that we have explored throughout this book, instructional leadership teams might also engage in the following tasks.

▸ Addressing concerns and answering questions about improvement plans from teachers and staff

▸ Monitoring student support programs and processes and recommending and assisting in making changes to these programs as needed

▸ Guiding and monitoring the work of collaborative teams, monitoring common assessments, reviewing the results of assessment processes, reviewing team goals, and keeping teams working toward the same outcomes

▸ Conducting goal-setting presentations and end-of-the-year progress reports with the superintendent and district-level leadership

▸ Working with teachers and staff to problem solve issues that arise during the school-turnaround process

▸ Building teacher capacity by designing and implementing professional development aligned to teacher needs

- ▸ Building in mental health opportunities within the school day

- ▸ Reviewing intervention programs and models to help students increase their academic achievement

- ▸ Conducting many other tasks that may be needed in the school-turnaround project

In a successful school-turnaround effort, the principal's role can change during the turnaround process. The principal may start by making the majority of the decisions involved in the turnaround but may gradually involve the instructional leadership team in making more decisions as the project is implemented. The timeline for this sort of transition can vary based on the culture of the school, the experience level of the team members, the comfort and confidence of the principal, and other factors. When a principal and a team work together to make a sound transition, it's very beneficial to the turnaround process. A strong and high-functioning instructional leadership team has been a crucial component in our work with school turnaround.

A sample agenda for an instructional leadership team meeting appears in figure 3.4.

Sample Agenda for Instructional Leadership Team

Meeting date: October 4

- Meeting opening and good news
- Review and update school-improvement goals and activities.
- Plan upcoming data and review school-improvement plan update for superintendent and selected central office staff.
- Discuss the teacher creed; review draft for clarification and refinement.
- Discuss upcoming data training for staff.
    - Plan small- and large-group sessions.
    - Make screencasts.
- Update on the development of a Google Doc where collaborative team information is posted (assessment results, collaborative team goals, teacher reflections, and other information related to student learning collaborative teams collect and gather)
- Fall conferences with families
    - Plan for reaching out to parents
    - Schedule and visit coordination
- Update on school-improvement goals
    - Information about the data warehouse for teachers
    - Assistance in reviewing and refining school-improvement goals
- Adjourn meeting.

Figure 3.4: Sample instructional leadership team meeting agenda.

Collaborative Teams

Collaborative teams are smaller groups of teachers organized by grade level, subject area, or some other common focus. In schools implementing turnaround efforts, collaborative teams are where the majority of the work and refinement of assessments, teaching strategies, and other teaching and learning modifications essential to the success of the turnaround effort take place. Some of the specific tasks collaborative teams perform to support turnaround include the following.

- ▸ Setting team goals that are aligned to and support the larger school-improvement or turnaround goals

- ▸ Supporting peers in improving their instruction and assessment skills

- ▸ Working in collaboration with the instructional leadership team to support the school-improvement effort

- ▸ Developing and administering common assessments

- ▸ Analyzing the results of common assessment data and developing intervention plans to address learning issues

- ▸ Planning and conducting extended or additional learning opportunities to help improve academic achievement for students

- ▸ Implementing the RTI process and other strategies for raising student achievement

- ▸ Assessing and refining goals to ensure a continued match with school-improvement goals

- ▸ Supporting each team member in setting and reaching professional growth goals

- ▸ Providing primary professional development support, such as observing one another teach and then providing feedback, sharing new instructional strategies, and coaching one another

- ▸ Ensuring all members of the team or group are working toward the success of the school-improvement plan

In school turnaround, the work of collaborative teams is important because it impacts the content and instructional strategies that are directly connected to student learning. It is at this team level that the turnaround leader and instructional leadership team need to provide the most support.

Building Operations Team

The building operations team is a team made up of staff members from various departments and job responsibilities that serves a unique function in the school-turnaround process. This team is involved in improving the appearance and cleanliness of the school and successfully managing other organizational processes, which can be important in supporting successful academic improvement. For example, if a turnaround school is working to improve schoolwide behavior management, a building operations team might be engaged in examining student traffic patterns to determine the most efficient way to move students between classes. The team might also provide input and direction to the staff on the schoolwide behavior expectations.

Building operations teams can assist in managing the following tasks.

▸ Reviewing facility maintenance issues and developing a schoolwide maintenance plan

▸ Examining the traffic flow and movement patterns within the school and providing recommendations for improving traffic flow

▸ Reviewing behavior-management data such as office referrals and common discipline issues and making recommendations for ways to help improve or enhance student behavior issues

▸ Reviewing and helping to refine mottos, mission statements, signage, and other communication materials for students, parents, and teachers

▸ Providing guidance in school remodeling plans to ensure student success

▸ Reviewing other facility-related aspects to increase the success of the school-turnaround project

Figure 3.5 shows a sample agenda from a building operations team meeting.

Sample Building Operations Team Meeting Agenda

- Good news and updates
- Report on schoolwide positive behavior initiative
- Review of front entrance cleaning project and student and staff maintenance process
- Discussion of custodial appreciation week plans
- Discussion of issues reported by faculty and committee members
- Items for discussion at next meeting
- Adjourn meeting.

Figure 3.5: Sample building operations team agenda.

The Student Intervention Team

Another way to distribute leadership and boost the success of a school-turnaround project is to create a student intervention team. Some schools might call this team the teacher assistance team or student assistance team, but we find it's helpful to use a title that is descriptive of the job the team actually does, which is providing interventions to help students increase their success at school.

Student intervention teams are usually comprised of teachers and other professionals who meet regularly to discuss learning and behavior issues in classrooms. During these discussions, the student intervention team members listen to the teacher describe the problem or situation, ask clarifying questions to better understand the situation, and then work with the teacher to develop an intervention plan to address the problems. During the planning process, team members also work with the teacher to develop assessments to gather data during the intervention. The team will later examine the data to gauge the effectiveness of the intervention plan implemented to improve the learning for the student.

Membership on the team is based on the expertise and availability of staff, plus student and teacher needs. Some of the most common members include:

- School psychologist
- Special education teacher
- Regular education teacher
- Reading teacher or specialist
- English language teacher
- Mathematics teacher
- A member of the administrative team

The student intervention team is a powerful part of a school-turnaround process because it builds on the collaborative power of colleagues working together to solve problems. Team members work together to plan interventions when those the collaborative team has designed and implemented haven't fully addressed issues. They also gather data to assess the effectiveness of the interventions. If the intervention plan is not working, the leader for the student intervention team quickly recognizes this and helps the teacher make adjustments to get the plan back on track.

Once the teacher has implemented the intervention plan for four to six weeks, the student intervention team schedules a follow-up meeting with the teacher. In this follow-up meeting, the teacher shares data related to the plan. The student intervention team members listen to the data presentation, and then share their thoughts about whether to refine the plan or continue with implementation as planned.

Members of the student intervention team need to be good at listening and understanding situations. They need to be able to withhold judgement while sharing possible ideas with the teacher. They also need to be able to coach and support teachers during plan implementation.

Figure 3.6 shows a sample of the process for student intervention team operations.

Student Intervention Team Process

1. Teacher or staff member becomes concerned about a student because of:

   - Academics
   - Behavior
   - Health
   - Social-emotional issues
   - Attendance

2. Teacher or staff member assesses the severity of the situation. If student is in danger of harm to self or others (behaving in an unsafe way or exhibiting emotional outbursts), report the situation directly to an administrator for appropriate action. Do not wait! Consult with the following as needed.

   - Principal
   - Student's dean
   - School psychologist
   - School nurse
   - School resource officer
   - Child crisis team
   - Child protective services

3. Once there is no longer concern for the safety of the student or others, the teacher or staff member completes the appropriate referral form and submits it to the student intervention team leader.

Figure 3.6: Sample operating procedures for a student intervention team.

Figure 3.7 shows a sample of a student intervention team flyer.

What Is a Student Intervention Team (SIT)?

The student intervention team is a problem-solving and coordinating structure that assists students, families, and teachers to develop positive solutions for maximizing student success. It provides an opportunity for school staff to present their concerns about an individual student, to plan a positive course of action through discussion and study, and then assign responsibilities and monitor results for a student.

Figure 3.7: Sample student intervention team information flyer.

Increasing Success With Supportive Structures

In addition to the primary team organizations we have discussed, there are several other supportive structures that help to increase the success of the turnaround process. One of these structures is a regular schedule of meetings that the principal has with the entire teaching staff.

Traditional faculty meetings in which the principal presents information and the rest of the faculty sit and listen do little to contribute to the development of skills teachers need to successfully engage in the turnaround process. Leaders must transform the traditional faculty meeting into a collaborative experience that is rich with authentic problem solving. This type of in-depth faculty meeting includes the following elements.

▸ Opportunities for faculty to work together and develop collaborative relationships

▸ Opportunities for faculty to get to know one another on a deeper level so they can access one another's strengths and develop interdependent relationships

▸ Celebrations of success

▸ Activities for whole-group problem solving

▸ Opportunities for addressing common professional development needs

▸ A forum in which group members can share their challenges, insights, and successes and offer one another support

In order to transform faculty meetings into learning and support opportunities, turnaround leaders implement specific activities and strategies during staff meetings. In *Energizing Staff Meetings* (Eller & Eller, 2006), we share a variety of strategies and ideas to help make faculty meetings collaborative, problem-solving opportunities. Following are some strategies we use most often in working successfully with faculty to flip schools.

▸ **Good news:** A powerful way to start faculty meetings off on a positive note. At the beginning of the meeting, ask volunteers to share a good news item that is either personal or professional. Good news sets a positive tone that carries through the rest of the meeting.

▸ **Music:** Another strategy that helps to set a positive tone is the use of music at the beginning of a meeting. Select songs that sooth, energize, motivate, and so on, depending on the mood you want to set. You can also use music to call people to the meeting or transition between processes.

- **Small-group brainstorming:** Rather than asking the entire faculty to develop ideas, randomly divide the faculty into small groups to brainstorm. Dividing into smaller groups ensures more participation by more staff members and gets more people involved in idea generation.

- **Visual processing strategies:** When faculty members can process visually, it helps take some of the emotion out of a decision. It's helpful to ask faculty members to discuss ideas in small groups and then write their ideas on paper or sticky notes and share them that way, or highlight them with a projector. By using posted ideas, teachers are able to have a more objective perspective and tend to not take things so personally during debate and discussion.

Helping Teachers Improve Their Instruction

A fundamental process in flipping or turning around a school is helping teachers improve their instruction. If students are not performing well, the first place (after classroom and schoolwide behavior management) to address is teaching and learning. Within the area of teaching and learning, several conditions may be impacting student achievement. They include:

- Ineffective teaching methods
- Lack of student motivation by the teacher
- Not teaching to the proper level of instruction for the students (the content level could be too low or too high)
- Not teaching to the standards (school, district, state, or national)
- The instruction not being relevant to the learners
- Lack of use of formative and summative assessment in making instructional decisions
- Teachers not building relationships with students

Once the instructional leadership team completes a data analysis of the conditions at the school, members should discuss and decide on what may be causing students' learning and achievement issues. In the following sections we provide strategies for addressing these conditions.

Teaching to Standards

For a school to be flipped or turned around, all teachers need to be teaching to an agreed-on set of standards. Since standards represent curriculum outcomes that are most important for the students to master, helping teachers identify, become familiar with, and align their teaching and assessment efforts to standards is crucial in a school-turnaround process.

The instructional leadership team works with grade-level or content-area collaborative teams to unpack standards. In unpacking standards, groups of teachers meet to discuss the standards in their content area, the academic content in these standards, and the skills students need to learn in each standard. A summary of a process for unpacking standards appears in figure 3.8.

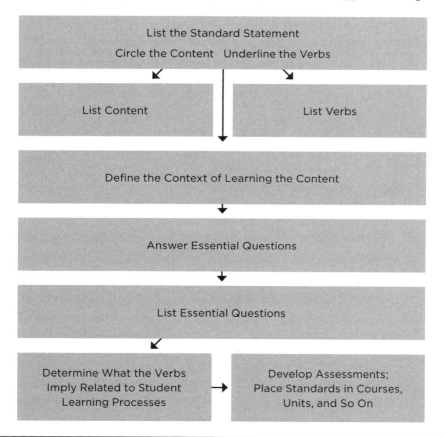

Figure 3.8: Process for unpacking standards.

By unpacking the standards, teachers understand the essential learning (content and process) they need to focus on in their classrooms. Unpacking and understanding standards help ensure everyone is teaching the most important content and processes and working together to support student learning.

Plan, Do, Study, Act Cycle

Once teams have defined the essential standards to be taught, teachers need to find ways to help them manage the learning in their classrooms. Using collaborative grade-level or subject-area teams for this process can be very helpful. Using the plan, do, study, act cycle (PDSA; figure 3.9) helps teachers work in collaboration to help each other be successful as teachers.

Preplan	Choose a focus for your team's plan, do, study, act cycle.
	Cycle Ideas:
	• Small goals aligned to your year-long collaborative team goal
	• Unit performance
	• Proficiency of a standard
	• Student connectedness
	• Student engagement
Plan	**What do we expect students to learn?**
	• Who already knows this and who does not? Consider using a preassessment.
	• What is your SMART goal for this cycle?
	How will we know they are learning?
	• What does success or proficiency look like?
	• How will we track the data?
	• How will we formatively assess progress toward the cycle goal? Create these formative assessments.
	• What student work will we analyze?
	How will we respond when they don't learn?
	• See the Act description for more details in this area.
	How will we respond if they already know it?
	• What strategies or teaching practices will we try throughout this cycle?
	• How will we engage students in the learning?
	• How will we differentiate?
Do	**What do we expect students to learn?**
	• Implement agreed-on strategies, teaching practices, and lesson plans.
	How will we know they are learning?
	• Use common formative assessments to measure progress toward cycle goal.
	How will we respond when they don't learn?
	• Implement differentiation plan based on preassessments.
	How will we respond if they already know it?
	• Implement enrichment plan.

Study	Did students learn what we expected them to learn? Which students did and which students did not?
	• Analyze student work and student data from common formative assessments.
	• Determine the impact of your teaching and the effectiveness of your strategies.
	• Decide which students still need support in reaching the goal and which students are ready for the next step.
	• What are the barriers impacting student performance? How can we remove these barriers?
Act	**Throughout the Cycle**
	• Respond to students who did not learn.
	• Try something different to help these students reach their goal.
	• Continue measuring progress through formative assessments.
	• Respond to students who already know it.
	• Provide opportunities for enrichment.
	At the End of the Cycle
	• What worked and what did not work throughout this cycle?
	• What practices will you continue to implement as a result of your data?
	• What practices will you refine, adjust, or abandon as a result of your data?
	• How will you refine, adjust, or abandon your practices?
Possible Structures Throughout the Cycle	
• Plan, Do, Study, Act	
• Plan, Do, Study, Act, Do, Study, Act, and so on	

Figure 3.9: The plan, do, study, act cycle.

Microteaching

Another strategy that is helpful in flipping or turning around a school related to improving teaching and learning is providing opportunities for teachers to help each identify and implement new teaching strategies. In this aspect, teachers get a chance to collaborate to solve problems and learn from each other. One strategy teachers have found helpful is microteaching.

Microteaching involves teachers recording a portion of their lessons, bringing the recordings to one of their regular collaborative team meetings, sharing the recordings, and getting feedback from their colleagues. In one school we have worked with, the practice of microteaching has become a part of the culture. In this school, teachers bring samples of their recordings to staff meetings to share with the colleagues and obtain feedback and ideas.

A System of Interventions

Making sure that students learn what they are supposed to learn so all students can achieve at high levels is a necessary part of any school-turnaround effort. Many schools use a formal model to implement and monitor their instruction and intervention. We have used the response to intervention model (RTI) with great success in schools in which we have worked. Entire books have been written about RTI (Buffum, 2017); in this book, we focus on RTI implementation as it relates to providing and tracking student learning interventions that support the school-turnaround process.

The RTI process includes three levels or tiers of instruction.

1. Tier 1 is best first instruction. This is the instruction that all students receive.

2. Tier 2 is targeted support for students who haven't learned in Tier 1.

3. Tier 3 is intensive support for students who still struggle after Tier 2 support.

The three tiers of RTI are often shown in an inverted pyramid to show the number of students each tier typically involves (figure 3.10).

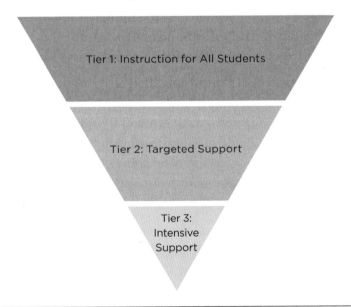

Figure 3.10: RTI pyramid of intervention.

Even though Tier 3 serves the smallest number of students, the interventions in this tier may take the most amount of time and effort to administer. In the following section, we show how RTI might be used in a school-turnaround effort.

Tier 1

At this level, the instructional leadership team and the principal leading a school turnaround would identify ways to make the core instruction and learning opportunities better for all students. If many students are experiencing difficulties in an area (a course, content area, concept, and so on) then improving instruction in that area should be a priority. The problem could be related to teachers' instructional methods, the level of difficulty of the content, or a variety of other factors. The instructional leadership team would work with collaborative teacher teams to determine the cause of the problem and how to address it.

Once the teams have worked to determine a solution, the instructional leadership team assists in assessing the area and measuring the impact of the change. If students are doing better, the change is working. If student achievement has not improved, the teams need to work to develop and implement another solution to address the issue.

Tier 2

At this level, interventions target students who have not learned or attained success in Tier 1 instruction. Tier 2 interventions could include accommodations, extended time, breaking content into smaller pieces, teaching the content in a different way, and other strategies that provide the students with additional chances to be successful. The instructional leadership team works with collaborative teacher teams to develop and implement supports at this tier, and then monitor student achievement to determine if additional support is required.

Tier 3

In Tier 3, the instructional leadership team works with grade-level or content-area collaborative teams to assist them in designing intensive interventions for a small number of students still struggling after Tier 2 interventions. Some of these interventions could include using audio text, reduced assignments, alternative learning targets, and other intensive interventions.

The three-tiered system in action might look something like this: once a teacher is aware a student is struggling after Tier 1 instruction and assessment of learning standards, that teacher first discusses the situation with his or her collaborative team. The team works with the teacher to determine at least two Tier 2 interventions to implement and assess. If after a two-week trial, the situation has not improved, the process moves to Tier 3 interventions. The school might have a SIT (student intervention team) in place to help the teacher identify or design a more intensive intervention, which is then implemented for a minimum of four weeks.

If at the end of the intervention, the issue has not improved, the student may be referred to the Learner Study Team or some other team designed to assess the student for possible special education support. This team further assists the teacher and may lead to special education or some other intensive assistance process.

Making Rituals, Ceremonies, and Celebrations a Priority

In our experiences flipping schools, we have found that rituals, ceremonies, and celebrations are essential for successful turnaround. Each process and special event should be meaningful to members of the school community, for both students and teachers. We offer the following suggestions (Eller & Eller, 2006).

Quarterly Celebrations

Choose accomplishments (either student, staff, or both) to celebrate each quarter and make celebration a habit. For example, allow students who have not had any tardies during the quarter to come to a common area (front entrance, lunchroom, and so on) for the last ten minutes of the day to get a reward, such as ice cream, fruit, or some other snack; a pencil or pen from the school store; a small stuffed animal (such as the school mascot); and other small things of interest to students. Other examples of quarterly celebrations could include the following.

▸ Invite a DJ to come in to school to play some of the students' favorite music or songs.

▸ Hold a "fun Friday" event, such as open gym time, open swim (if you have a pool), open computer lab (for games), board game time, and open library time for students who want a quiet place to read. All of these open times could be happening simultaneously so students can choose which activity they'd like to attend.

▸ Offer karaoke so students can sign in and perform or listen to music.

▸ Offer an ice cream bar session in the lunchroom. Students who meet the criteria for the award can come down and have an ice cream bar.

All of these quarterly celebrations are based on student interest and choice. The student voice committee, the student council, or some other student group can help determine the quarterly celebration options.

Alternative Learning Days

Alternative learning days are days when regular classes are not held. Instead, the school offers alternative courses. These courses can last an entire day (students choose only one) or they can last an hour (students choose more than one). Teachers generate ideas for courses from their hobbies and interests. Examples of courses include fishing, snow shoeing, conducting insect studies, game sessions, and so on. Those teachers not interested in teaching a course can help with logistical elements of the alternative learning day.

Banana Celebration

At some point in the school year when some of the turnaround projects are starting to yield positive results, the principal puts a banana in each staff member's mailbox along with a note asking teachers to decorate them and bring them to the upcoming staff meeting. During the first part of the meeting, staff members are encouraged to share their decorated bananas. After this activity is complete, the school leader or members of the instructional leadership team reveal the good news related to the school-improvement or turnaround plan. They unveil buckets of ice cream and encourage staff members to make celebration sundaes with their bananas. Once they have made the sundaes, they celebrate the accomplishments as they eat their sundaes and visit with their colleagues.

Chapter Summary

Earlier in this chapter, we introduced you to a scenario that shows Principal Roberta Evans discovering that the use of teacher collaborative teams helps make the process of school turnaround successful. Let's now look at a scenario that shows how the use of collaborative teams has a positive impact on the success of the turnaround plan at Round Lake School.

As Principal Michelle Lee reviews the data related to student success at Round Lake Middle School, she notices a significant decrease in the number of office referrals for student behavior issues. She thinks that the decrease might be the result of the work of teams within the school. She decides to seek out more information to determine what may have led to the decrease.

She conducts some informal, individual conversations with teachers and asks them to share their perceptions on the impact the teams are having on the school. Several teachers tell her how helpful it is to have a place to go (the student intervention team) when they are experiencing difficulties and don't know what to do. They explain that the student intervention team members always listen and help them understand the core of the issue in question. Then, members help them develop and measure an intervention plan. The planning and measuring are part of a process that the teachers find very helpful.

Several other teachers report that the reflection council has also been a valuable resource for helping manage some of the issues related to student behavior. They say that the reflection council really helps students take ownership for and work to resolve their issues. These teachers also say that they have started to notice a transfer of the skills the students use in the reflection council. The teachers see the students implementing the skills in classrooms and in their interactions with their peers.

The feedback that Principal Lee receives in these informal conversations with teachers confirms her choice to develop teacher leadership in her school using teaming structures. She finds that the teacher teams have a lot of credibility in the school, and that the teams are able to proactively address issues administration members previously handled. Teachers taking responsibility for implementing team-determined strategies builds capacity more than if administration had prescribed the steps to take. In the long run, teacher ownership and collaboration have a strong positive impact on the school and on its turnaround effort.

In this chapter, we examined the power of distributing leadership and building structures to boost teacher ownership and engagement. We also talked about additional supportive structures for teachers and processes to support teachers in improving instruction. We then described how celebrations, ceremonies, and rituals can support positive growth for both teachers and students. We hope that our perspectives will help you leverage the creative and leadership potential of the staff at your school, and that processing and celebrating important experiences will help propel your own school-turnaround journey.

Reflection Questions

As you reflect on the content of this chapter, answer the following questions.

1. What is the benefit of developing teacher leadership through the use of different types of teaming structures in a school-turnaround project?

2. What are the areas that an instructional leadership team helps to manage? How can they work to develop communication with staff?

3. How can a reflective council help to build responsibility in students? What are some of the characteristics of the teachers who could serve on a reflective council?

4. What strategies for helping teachers improve their instruction seem best suited for use in your school?

5. How do you currently celebrate in your school, and what additional structures and practices could you celebrate?

Chapter 4

Assessing and Developing Your Leadership Skills

Lester Davis, a middle school principal, has been hired to lead a failing school. After he assesses the situation, he develops a plan that involves the implementation of an instructional leadership team. This team is responsible for working with faculty to gather their ideas and opinions related to the school change process. Each member of the instructional leadership team represents a certain group or department at the school.

Most faculty members voice their opinions about key decisions during team discussions and then agree to follow the team's recommendations once decisions are made. If problems arise during implementation, faculty members share their concerns with members of the team.

However, one faculty member, Diane, does not follow recommendations in her classroom. During meetings with the team, she engages in unrelated conversations, and more than a few times she attempts to undermine a decision by making comments like, "I'm not doing that," or "I've tried that in the past, and it didn't work." At first, Diane says these things discreetly with her closest allies at the school, but as implementation continues, Diane becomes bolder and begins confronting school-leadership team members.

Several team members inform Principal Davis of the situation. He knows he will have to get the situation under control.

Principal Davis sends Diane an email asking her to meet with him at the end of the day. At the start of the meeting, Principal Davis shares the purpose and the agenda for the conversation. As he communicates the issues to Diane, he focuses on behaviors that he has seen rather than on those other faculty have reported to him.

He knows that if he focuses on observable behaviors it will be hard for Diane to refute his points.

Principal Davis tells Diane that he has heard her make negative comments about implementing the exit tickets in her classroom. He reminds her that having all teachers use the exit tickets was decided by the instructional leadership team. He asks Diane why she has been making negative comments. Diane replies that she tried this strategy in the past and it didn't work. She shares that she is skeptical about trying it again.

Principal Davis tells Diane that in spite of her skepticism, she needs to implement exit tickets in her classroom. He tells Diane that implementing common strategies helps the students understand the strategies and experience clear, common expectations. These common expectations provide a foundation to support their learning.

At the end of the conference, he shares he'll be happy to provide some assistance for her if she needs it to be able to implement the strategy in her classroom. He reminds Diane that he'll be looking for her use of exit tickets when he does his weekly walkthrough visits to her class. At the end of the meeting, Principal Davis checks to make sure Diane understands his expectations and to determine if she needs any support to implement exit tickets. Diane says that she knows she needs to try the exit tickets again and that she'll let him know if she needs any assistance to do it successfully.

In this example, we see how Principal Davis needed to meet with Diane to make sure she followed the instructional leadership team's mandated plan. While leaders of school-turnaround efforts would like to show support for teacher autonomy, they must support non-negotiable, schoolwide improvement efforts designed to change the learning environment.

When faculty members like Diane are either unable or unwilling to honor non-negotiable agreements, leaders must have the skill to find out the source of the resistance. Is it because the teacher doesn't know how to implement what is required, or is the teacher unwilling to implement the required process? It's helpful to meet with a teacher who is resistant to the decisions of the team to understand his or her perspective. Once the leader has done this, he or she can then help the teacher understand the importance of the practice and develop a plan to implement it. When working with people who are not on board or resistant to the school-improvement plan, a leader may also need to followup to help the teacher to implement the requirement.

Leading a school-turnaround effort requires a focus on a different set of leadership skills from those required to lead a school that is already doing well or even just working on a less-urgent improvement effort. These skills or competencies enable a principal to perform the tasks needed to successfully flip the school. In this chapter, we look at these necessary competencies. We explore how leaders can use different power bases to lead their staff. We also describe the types of difficult and resistant staff that can impede leadership. We show strategies to effectively deal with these staff members and how what we call the *care factor* can help manage turnaround. Finally, we discuss the grief process and how it can apply to selective turnaround.

Leadership Competencies for School Turnaround

Julie Kowal and Joe Ableidinger (2011) approach leadership of turnaround schools from a business perspective. They compare the leadership behaviors of a turnaround principal to those of startup company leaders. Like a startup company, a turnaround school is changing the status quo, so Kowal and Ableidinger (2011) point out that many of the leadership needs are similar. For example, a turnaround school may be restructured like a startup company is new. Both will need to monitor and adjust their implementation based on their analysis of results. In their analysis of leadership needs of turnaround schools, Kowal and Ableidinger (2011) offer the following leadership strategies.

▸ **Driving for results:** The turnaround leader needs a strong desire to achieve outstanding results and a commitment to the task-oriented actions that success requires.

▸ **Influencing for results:** Turnaround leaders cannot accomplish change alone. They must rely on the work of others. A successful turnaround leader can motivate others and influence their thinking and behavior to obtain results.

▸ **Engaging in problem solving:** Turnaround leaders use data analysis to inform decisions, make clear, logical plans that others can follow, and ensure a strong connection between school learning goals and classroom activity.

▸ **Showing confidence to lead:** The leader stays visibly focused, committed, and self-assured despite personal and professional challenges common when flipping a school.

While research has established that certain leadership competencies contribute toward successful school turnaround, it is also important for leaders to assess and develop their own competencies. Figure 4.1 (page 70) provides an opportunity to reflect on your own competencies in relation to those Kowal and Ableidinger (2011) outline.

Directions: School leaders need to possess a set of competencies in order to successfully lead turnaround efforts. Use this worksheet to reflect on your skill set to determine where you are strong and where you would benefit from further development.

Leadership Competency	Competency Attributes	My Areas of Strength and Areas for Further Development
Driving for results	Strong desire to achieve outstanding results and the task-oriented actions required for success	Strengths: Areas for further development:
Influencing for results	Ability to motivate others and influence their thinking and behavior to obtain results	Strengths: Areas for further development:
Engaging in problem solving	Ability to analyze data, make informed decisions, and develop clear and logical plans Ability to ensure a strong connection between school learning goals and classroom activity	Strengths: Areas for further development:
Showing confidence to lead	Ability to stay visibly focused, committed, and self-assured to withstand the personal and professional challenges common during turnaround	Strengths: Areas for further development:

What are some of the patterns you notice as you reflect on your strengths and areas for further development? How will you use your strengths for successful turnaround? What will you do to address areas in which you need further development?

Figure 4.1: Assessing your turnaround competencies.

*Visit **go.SolutionTree.com/schoolimprovement** for a free reproducible version of this figure.*

Let's see how Veronica Gray, a high school principal, articulates and uses competencies in leading her school.

Principal Veronica Gray has been working on a turnaround effort at Keshawn High School for two years. She entered this effort well aware of certain established competencies that the effort would require, but she also developed her own competencies through assessment of herself and those she leads. When she was named principal, she took the opportunity to meet with each staff member in the summer prior to starting her position to get to know them and understand the perceptions that each has of the school. She came away from these meetings with a sense that teachers and staff felt they were being attacked and that their efforts diminished under the leadership of the previous principal. After speaking with teachers, she understands how the previous principal's approach made people feel unappreciated and undervalued. She knows from research and experience that validating the efforts of staff is a key competency of successful turnaround leadership, but now she realizes she will have to make an extra effort to communicate staff importance and use encouragement as her first strategy to help build confidence. Principal Gray utilizes previous knowledge of leadership competencies and develops a new understanding of required competencies through an analysis of her work with staff at her school.

At each staff meeting, and in most of her communications to teachers and staff, Principal Gray uses encouragement when driving for results. She reminds teachers of how far they have come in their journey and of how hard they have worked to make gains. She sets high expectations but uses positive encouragement to move staff forward. She constantly reminds staff of the larger school-turnaround goals, using encouragement rather than pressure to keep them moving forward on these goals.

Principal Gray uses the positive relationships she nurtured to influence teachers to implement new strategies and techniques. Most teachers try the new ideas because they respect Principal Gray's efforts, not because she is in charge and can tell them what to do.

Whenever there is a challenge or problem, Principal Gray uses it as an opportunity to engage staff in collaborative work to develop a plan to address the challenge or problem. She first models how to effectively collaborate before teachers set out in their collaborative teams. Because of this collaborative effort, staff feel involved and gain confidence in their abilities to solve problems.

Even though she privately experiences some self-doubt, Principal Gray publicly approaches her leadership tasks with confidence. She shows a can do attitude and works with staff to address issues as they arise. As a result of her confidence, staff members' confidence increases, and they are more likely to feel confident in the school-turnaround process.

Principal Gray personalized and tailored her leadership skills to match the needs of the school. By taking stock of your leadership competencies, you can implement plans that utilize your existing competencies while allowing you to grow and develop in other areas. In addition to understanding and developing these leadership competencies, turnaround leaders should also understand the dynamic between leadership and power bases, and how the choice of how to lead will affect motivation of staff members and ultimately affect the success of the turnaround effort.

Optimal Level of Leadership Intervention

As the leader of school turnaround, it's crucial to be able to determine the amount of influence or leadership intervention staff require, and then apply the optimal amount. Sometimes, leaders have difficulty with this concept if they tend to take a one-size-fits-all approach to leadership. A one-size-fits-all approach is often not ideal, as it can lead to providing too little assistance for some and too much for others.

Like doctors in the field of health and medicine, leaders of school turnaround must be aware of the importance of providing unique guidance and intervention to keep staff and projects healthy.

Following are some points to take into consideration when determining the proper level of intervention to maximize success in a school-turnaround project.

- ▸ **The culture or working climate at the school:** If the school culture is positive and collaborative, staff members may more readily take on some of the responsibility for school improvement. If the culture is full of negativity or is poorly established, they may not be so eager. Teachers and staff from cultures that contain negativity or that do not have well-established norms require more intervention to help them move forward.

- ▸ **The number of past intervention attempts:** If the school has tried many strategies for turnaround but failed, you may need to provide attention and be more engaged in the interventions. If the school has not experienced failed ideas, you may be able to let teams do more on their own with support and guidance.

- ▸ **The severity of the situation:** For major changes, you may have to provide more guidance when implementing more comprehensive interventions. You and the instructional leadership team may want to break the change into small parts, and build in regular checkpoints so you can see how things are going. If the necessary changes are smaller or more incremental, you may be able to rely more on team leadership. It may be possible to manage these types of changes by grade-level or content-area collaborative groups. You or the instructional leadership team may only need to check on progress periodically.

▸ **The number of people involved with the intervention:** If interventions focus on a small group, such as a department or grade level, you can use less-comprehensive strategies to support the change. If the entire school staff must make changes, you may want to coordinate the comprehensive approach when supporting changes.

▸ **The influence of informal teacher leaders:** In schools where productive, informal teacher leadership exists, principals find they can use less-comprehensive interventions, since teachers are also helping. In situations where either no productive, informal teacher leadership exists or negative informal teacher leadership is present, you may need to employ stronger, more comprehensive leadership strategies.

▸ **The types of difficult or resistant staff members at the school:** The level of intervention is also determined by the number and types of difficult and resistant staff within a building. In the following section, we explore the types of difficult and resistant staff and their impact on your leadership style.

Difficult and Resistant Staff Members and Their Impact on Leadership

In our book, *Working With Difficult and Resistant Staff* (Eller & Eller, 2011), we describe eight staff member types and the difficulties they may cause in a school. Here, we provide a brief overview of these eight types of difficult and resistant staff members and how they might affect a school-turnaround project.

1. **Underminers:** The underminers are a group that works to undo proposed changes you or your instructional leadership team have instituted. They are dangerous to the school-turnaround effort since they may actively work to stop progress and move the school backward to its former practices.

2. **Contrarians:** Contrarians are staff members who always seem to be on the opposite side of every issue. They are harmful to the school-turnaround process because they consistently voice (either openly or covertly) an opposing view. Contrarians may be well-versed and informed in their opposition so they may influence others to go along with them. They may be able to negatively influence a critical mass of staff and derail the school-turnaround process.

3. **Recruiters:** Recruiters are staff members who hold negative views and try to get others on their side. Recruiters may target less-confident or impressionable staff members to join their side. Similar to the contrarians, they can use their recruiting skills to build a critical mass opposed to the school-turnaround plan.

4. **Challenged:** The challenged are a group that may not have the knowledge or skills to implement the strategies and techniques turnaround requires, but have a hard time admitting it. Because these staff members lack the knowledge to implement the required changes, their lower ability levels may hold back others who are moving forward on productive initiatives.

5. **On-the-job retirees:** On-the-job retirees are people who seem to be trying to coast or wait out the proposed changes. These staff members can be detrimental to the school-turnaround process because they can have a significant influence on the school's working climate and culture.

6. **Resident experts:** Resident experts are people who think they have a lot of knowledge about the strategies and techniques you are requiring, but in reality, don't. These difficult staff types can be harmful to your school-turnaround efforts because their abilities to sound knowledgeable (when they are not) can undermine the confidence and commitment of the remaining staff members. They may cause staff members to question elements of the school-turnaround plan.

7. **Unelected representatives:** The unelected representatives are a group that wants to speak for others on the staff. In reality, they may not have the approval to do so. Since unelected representatives tend to speak up at meetings, they can turn conversations toward the negative. Also, unelected representatives make other staff members believe that what they say is what the majority of staff members believes. If a leader doesn't confront unelected representative behavior, staff may abandon or not follow through with the school-turnaround plan because they think others are opposed to it.

8. **Whiners and complainers:** Whiners and complainers are staff members who find the negative in everything. They will openly voice their opinions about how difficult something is or why it won't work. They can cause harm to school-turnaround plans because they are vocal in their complaints about everything related to the school-turnaround process.

Difficult and Resistant Staff and School Turnaround

As you move forward with school turnaround, you will want to identify potential issues that may slow or undermine your plan. One such issue is difficult and resistant staff. Use the worksheet in figure 4.2 to identify difficult staff members who might be resistant to change.

Directions: To address any problems difficult and resistant staff members present to your school-turnaround plan, it is important to first identify them and their impact on your building or district. The following worksheet will help you in completing this task. Review each of the major categories in the column on the left. Then write the names of any staff members and their actions that place them in the category. Finally, outline the impact these staff members have on your organization. You will use this information as you begin to generate your plan to work with these difficult and resistant people.

Difficult and Resistant Category	Staff Members in Category and Why	Impact on Organization
Underminers		
Contrarians		
Recruiters		
Challenged		
On-the-Job Retirees		
Resident Experts		
Unelected Representatives		
Whiners and Complainers		

What trends or patterns did you notice as you completed the template?

How strong are these difficult and resistant staff members?

How do you think you might start to address their behaviors?

Source: Eller & Eller, 2011.

Figure 4.2: Assessing your organization's difficult and resistant staff.

*Visit **go.SolutionTree.com/schoolimprovement** for a free reproducible version of this figure.*

Once you have identified some of the difficult and resistant staff members, you will want to develop plans to address their challenging behaviors. You may be able to address their difficulties through the normal supervision process, or you may need to develop an improvement plan to address these issues.

In our work, we have found that leading with what we call the *care factor*—showing teachers that you value them and their efforts—can go a long way in moving the school forward in the turnaround process.

The Care Factor

With the laser-like focus on student success in turnaround schools, it's easy to forget to think about staff needs; one of these needs is acceptance by the leader, to know that the leader cares about individual teachers and staff members—not just about test scores.

Let's see how leading with the care factor affects the interaction between Principal Quyen Pham and one of the teachers in her high school.

> Quyen Pham, the principal of Chavez High School, makes a point to let her staff know that they are important and that she cares for them. She gets to know each staff member on a personal level and acknowledges some of their strengths (both personally and professionally). Principal Pham understands that for teachers to be able to care for their students, they need to be cared for as well. In her leadership practices, she respects her staff and understands that they bring more to the school than just their professional skills and beliefs.
>
> Principal Pham discovers that Bill, a mathematics teacher, is upset after a mathematics collaborative team meeting in which he voiced negative opinions about the improvement strategies the school instructional leadership team had designed for teacher implementation. Bill shares that he is frustrated because he doesn't believe in the strategies the instructional leadership team has suggested and is not planning to follow through with the reteaching strategies the rest of the team will be employing after compiling the assessment results.
>
> Principal Pham sends Bill an email asking to meet with him. At the meeting, she tells Bill she heard that he was frustrated with the reteaching process. She shares an overview of the agenda for the meeting that includes the following.
>
> She gives Bill an opportunity to share his frustrations. She then shares the rationale for why the instructional leadership team selected the interventions. Together, they explore ways that Bill could be successful in working through the frustrations he expressed in order to implement the necessary interventions.
>
> They develop a plan for Bill to implement the strategies and for Principal Pham to support him in his efforts. During the conversation, Bill shares his frustrations and Principal Pham determines how she can work with Bill to meet his needs while he

implements the required interventions. Bill feels that the principal cares about him, but he also understands the need to make sure that he meets the same expectations as the rest of the faculty.

In this scenario, we see how Principal Pham uses the care factor to respond to Bill on a personal and emotional level. If Principal Pham had simply directed Bill to implement the interventions, Bill might have agreed in her presence but then worked half-heartedly at implementation. He could also have undermined Principal Pham with the rest of his team members by trying to recruit other teachers to object to the strategies, discouraging his colleagues to try the ideas, or trying to communicate with school board members or community members about his aversion to the strategies.

Instead, she built a good relationship with Bill, and he knew that she would help him, but that he needed to meet the same standards as the rest of the faculty. By listening to his frustrations and reasoning, she communicated that she cared.

The care factor makes sense to many leaders, however, other leaders think showing they care about staff members will make them appear too nice or wishy-washy. For example, when a leader takes the time to meet with and listen to a teacher's objections, some staff members may think the leader is not strong, otherwise he or she would just make the teacher comply. In the end, the leader may have to direct the teacher to implement the strategy, but listening shows that the leader cares enough to find out why there is an issue. Leaders utilizing the care factor with staff can communicate high expectations for performance while also showing care and support.

The Care Factor and Staff

Here are some strategies to use to develop the care factor with staff members.

▸ **Spend time getting to know staff members as whole people:** Teachers and other staff members have lives outside of school. By taking the time to get to know some of their outside interests and abilities, you may learn details that will help motivate and support them. Periodically meeting with staff members to see how things are going, talking with them to learn more about them, their passions, their families, and other aspects of their lives can let them know you care about them as people.

▸ **Find easy and inexpensive ways to show staff members you care about them:** Offer to cover a class for a teacher so she can attend a mid-day performance at her child's school, or allow a teacher to come in a few minutes late in the morning so he can attend a doctor's appointment with a loved one. Such small efforts can add up when working with others.

▸ **Ask your teachers and staff about family (when appropriate):** Show an interest in staff members and their lives outside the school setting. Listening as they share information about their families and personal lives is appropriate. Prying or asking them very personal questions is not appropriate.

▸ **Encourage staff to take advantage of new opportunities:** If an opportunity arises that fits the skill or interest of a particular staff member, alert the person to the opportunity. For example, encouraging a teacher to pursue an advanced degree or to consider working with a student teacher, serving as a mentor to a new colleague, or presenting at a conference are all ways to encourage growth. Show staff you care about their growth and development and understand their interests and goals.

▸ **Share the positive attributes of staff members when talking with them:** Communicate with staff that you notice and appreciate their strengths. People often focus on their limitations. When a leader sees something positive in a staff member, he or she should share that observation with the staff member. When you point out positive things people do, they get the message that you are looking for the positive in them. This also communicates caring.

In addition to exhibiting the care factor with teachers and other staff members, successful turnaround leaders show the care factor with students.

The Care Factor and Students

Turnaround leaders make students and families a top priority and show a genuine interest in them, which can go a long way in motivating students. Principals of successful turnaround efforts find ways to let students know their teachers and principal care for them by employing behaviors such as those outlined in the following list.

▸ Know students by name, and use their names when you talk with them.

▸ Greet students at the entrance of the school in the morning.

▸ Ask students how they are doing and what's happening in their lives.

▸ When visiting classrooms for walkthroughs, notice what students are working on and make positive comments about their work.

▸ Recognize when students are following guidelines and procedures and comment about their success.

Utilizing the care factor in your leadership of a turnaround school will go far in cementing your ability to motivate change and model for teachers and staff something they should consider doing with their students. Keep in mind, however, that school turnaround can be emotionally difficult for both staff members and leaders. In fact, some say that the turnaround process can cause feelings of grief similar to those people experience when they lose someone of significance.

Leadership Skills and the Grief Process

In her landmark book *On Death and Dying*, Swiss psychiatrist Elisabeth Kübler-Ross (2014) identifies five stages of grief: (1) denial, (2) anger, (3) bargaining, (4) depression, and (5) acceptance. This information may be helpful to you as you flip your school. Here is an overview of the five stages of grief as they might appear in a school-turnaround project.

1. **Denial:** Typically, a school community is aware if it has been identified as failing or has significant enough issues to warrant a turnaround. Reactions to the news can vary. It's common for staff to blame students, families, leadership, and bad data for the school's shortcomings.

2. **Anger:** The next stage that school stakeholders go through is anger. People get upset that the situation has happened to them. They might manifest their anger outwardly by verbalizing their frustration or inwardly by shutting down. Some will direct anger at the entity responsible for the failing designation, while others direct it at colleagues, and at leadership or administration. Even though this anger seems irrational, it is real and can be difficult to deal with as a leader.

3. **Bargaining:** Once school stakeholders work through their initial anger, they may move into the bargaining stage. In this stage, members may try to offer up deals to avoid the consequences of the school-turnaround situation. Members might say, "We'll work harder next year if . . ." or "Can you tell the state that we'll . . . if . . ." In most cases, being in need of turnaround is non-negotiable, so no amount of bargaining will change the situation.

4. **Depression:** Another stage that may have an impact on a school group is the depression phase. In this stage, people can become sad, easily upset, and may even shut down and quit trying. This stage can be dangerous since turnaround leaders will need to get

maximum commitment and effort from staff during the school-turnaround process.

5. **Acceptance:** After some time, people tend to accept the fact that their school is slated for turnaround. In the acceptance phase, staff members can be more open to the plans and changes that will be put in place for the school-turnaround effort.

It can be helpful for school-turnaround leaders to possess knowledge about the grieving process. When leaders can anticipate what might happen next, they are better able to deal with emotional reactions. Leaders might also discuss the stages of the grieving process with staff members, so that the staff members understand that the feelings they are experiencing are normal and expected. However, understanding the stages does not give staff members an excuse for being negative during the turnaround project. Don't allow comments like, "Well, I'm in the denial phase, so I should be hard to work with" or "I'm in the anger phase, so stay away from me." It's important to communicate understanding while also helping the person move forward. For example, saying something like, "I know this is hard for you. How can I help you get through this process?" lets him or her know you care but want to help him or her get back on track.

Turnaround leaders should provide some opportunities, such as those that follow, for staff to work through the five stages.

▸ **Open up meetings for staff conversation:** Open meetings that allow time for staff to share their concerns help release some of the pressure and anxiety associated with the grieving process. Principals must be careful not to let these meetings get out of control. Also, principals should provide opportunities for teachers and staff to develop strategies and plans to address concerns.

▸ **Outside professionals for staff assistance:** Some principals find that engaging outside professionals such as psychologists and counselors is a valuable way to help staff members work through the various grieving phases.

▸ **Rituals:** In some settings, school leaders have found great value in providing staff members with rituals to help them empty the negative emotions associated with the grieving phases. Some rituals might include writing down the positives and negatives of the old practice, letting everyone share and discuss them, putting them in a container, and burying them on the school grounds. Rituals like this help people to empty their emotions about old practices and move on.

Most important, promoting understanding of the grief stages gives leaders a way to guide staff members toward expressions of emotion through healthy means instead of getting upset. For example, letting someone share the issues they are facing can give him or her an outlet to "get it off their chest." Principals can work to manage stress levels and avoid total staff frustration.

As the leader of a turnaround school, you may encounter a staff made up of people who are at different stages of the grieving process at a given time. It will be important to be able to recognize behaviors associated with the stages that we presented earlier in this chapter. Consider the following set of skills as you deal with people in your turnaround effort.

- **Listen carefully:** Careful listening helps leaders understand the central issue or core of a person's concerns.

- **Don't take negative comments and actions personally:** If you become emotionally engaged, you may not be able to problem solve the situation and develop strategies to deal with it.

- **Know when a situation is getting out of control:** It can be a positive step for people to openly express their emotions. Emotions can get out of control, however, and people can become hostile. Leaders should be aware of when this is happening and take measures to lower the level of emotion and anger.

- **Think on your feet:** Situations that need to be addressed immediately will arise within teams and with individuals. For example, if you are leading a staff meeting and someone becomes upset, you may need to stop and address the situation immediately. If you are conducting a conference with a teacher and he or she brings up an issue that's not directly related to your conversation, you may need to stop to address the area of concern. Leaders must use their judgement in addressing different situations. Being able to quickly assess situations and develop possible strategies to deal with them is essential. Sometimes it will be impossible for a leader to respond immediately. For example, if you are conducting a staff meeting and someone becomes upset and starts making negative comments, you may not be able to stop to address the situation. You'll need to let the person know you hear his or her concern but are unable to stop to address it at this time. You can meet with him or her later to address the situation.

- **Confront people about negative comments and actions:** During grief phases, staff can and will make negative comments and do negative things, some of which will require confrontation. If someone makes a negative comment to you, you may need to address the issue right away. Letting someone know you heard the comment, telling him or her it's not appropriate, and directing him or her to not do it again are strategies you may choose to employ. If you don't confront such behavior, staff members will think the behavior is acceptable and perhaps question your ability to lead.

▸ **Rephrase comments, keeping the original meaning intact:** When people feel they are being listened to, it can help de-escalate tense emotions. When leaders can pause, listen, and repeat back what someone has said, the staff member feels validated and valued.

▸ **Understand the grief stages:** Having the ability to recognize the grief phases can help you determine how to help staff members move along on the continuum to acceptance. It also helps leaders see that the end is in sight. Knowing that a majority of the faculty has passed through a certain stage and is getting nearer to acceptance can help you get through difficult days.

Figure 4.3 provides a worksheet to rate your abilities to successfully navigate the grief stages.

Chapter Summary

Earlier in this chapter, we examined a scenario involving Lester Davis, the school principal, and Diane, a teacher who purposely undermined his decisions and the decisions of the instructional leadership team. Let's move ahead a few months and see their progress.

Principal Davis knows that he will have to check in with Diane regularly to make sure she follows expectations. He puts a weekly reminder in his calendar to stop by Diane's classroom to observe her implementation. He varies the timing of his visits to observe Diane at different times in different lessons. He also meets with Diane periodically to follow up with her on her progress.

His hard work begins to pay off as they move into the second semester. Diane's attitude changes. She sees the positive impact the turnaround strategies are having in her classroom. In a meeting with Principal Davis at the end of the third quarter, she thanks him for caring enough about her to help her improve her teaching. It would have been easy for the principal to simply reprimand her behavior, she notes. Instead, Principal Davis made sure Diane was successful.

Required Skill	Your Level of Skill E = Emerging C = Competent P = Proficient	Evidence for Rating	Strategy or Resource for Increasing Skill or Confidence in This Area
Listen carefully.			
Don't take negative comments and actions personally.			
Know when a situation is getting out of control.			
Think on your feet.			
Confront people about negative comments and actions.			
Rephrase comments, keeping the original meaning intact.			
Rephrase comments, keeping the original meaning intact.			
Understand the grief stages.			

Figure 4.3: Assessing your skills related to the grief process.

*Visit **go.SolutionTree.com/schoolimprovement** for a free reproducible version of this figure.*

Not every case of dealing with difficult or resistant staff ends like this one. While it wasn't easy for Diane to modify her attitude and consider strategy suggestions with an open mind, she did so, and her motivation came partly from recognizing and appreciating the work Principal Davis did to help her get on track. She felt good to learn something new that worked so well in her classroom. If Principal Davis had relied only on directives, Diane may have become more resistant to change and wouldn't have developed valuable new skills.

In this chapter, we examined elements that are key to helping principals understand and maximize their leadership styles. Understanding your preferred leadership style is important for your success in a turnaround effort. In addition, learning how to add strategies and modify your leadership behavior to match the needs of your school will help you be successful in your efforts.

In the next chapter, we explore how to gather and analyze important data to let you know exactly what the problems are that are causing your school to fail. Once you understand the causes, you can develop a plan to begin to address them.

Reflection Questions

As you reflect on the content of this chapter, answer the following questions.

1. How can understanding your leadership strengths and preferences assist you as you lead a school through the turnaround process?

2. Why is it important to consider the needs of the school in focusing on specific leadership strategies?

3. What did you learn in this chapter that can help you work more positively with your staff members?

4. How do you plan to implement what you've learned in this chapter?

Chapter 5

Gathering Data About Your School

As he prepares to start the school year, Principal Miguel Martinez spends considerable time reviewing data about his middle school. After reviewing current assessment information, he discovers that a significant number of students in certain subgroups (Latinos, African Americans, free- and reduced-lunch students, and students new to the country) is performing below expectation in mathematics and language arts. Moreover, Principal Martinez knows that there is likely more to be concerned about than these academic shortcomings.

Principal Martinez decides to complete a comprehensive assessment of the school for a variety of indicators of success. In addition to the mathematics and language arts testing information, he looks at discipline referrals, student attendance data, a summary of teachers' grades for the previous two years, and the number of parental contacts during the previous school year. The additional data give Principal Martinez a more comprehensive picture of the school. Instead of just understanding test scores, he sees patterns that provide further information about the school.

Using the information he gleans, Principal Martinez develops some initial ideas about a school-improvement plan. He knows he needs to get others involved in understanding the issues the school faces. He decides to call a meeting with an existing building team—the instructional leadership team—and plans a two-day data retreat to review the assessment information and make recommendations about a school-improvement plan. He has some funding available to pay the team members for their time.

At the initial team meeting, Principal Martinez shares the data he analyzed to draw his conclusions. Then he asks the team to identify other sources of information they think should be considered before developing the school-improvement plan. They suggest he add the number of English learners, student attendance rates, the mobility rate, data related to family makeup, and the percentage of special needs students in each classroom. They think this additional information will better help them understand student needs.

Principal Martinez knows he will have to conduct follow-up observations to assess the specific teaching strategies staff members employ. He will also need to determine which high-impact strategies he should recommend teachers begin to implement. With the addition of follow-up observations and continued refinement, he will need to determine if the instruction is getting better or if he needs to consider working with the team to develop a school-turnaround plan.

By taking time to understand all aspects of his school's performance, Principal Martinez was gathering and analyzing data to determine the need for further steps. In this chapter, we address how school leaders can guide data gathering and analysis for their use in creating a school-improvement plan. We cover how to develop an initial data-gathering plan, form a data-analysis team, train the team to gather and analyze data, begin the data-gathering process for different types of data, and use methods to gather alternative data about school culture important to the school-turnaround process.

Developing an Initial Data-Gathering Plan

An important element to the success of a data-analysis process is a comprehensive and coherent plan for gathering data. In their book, *Turning Your School Around: A Self-Guided Audit for School Improvement*, Robert D. Barr and Debra L. Yates (2010) provide the sound foundation for planning a data-gathering and analysis process. They suggest the following six steps to include in a school-level plan.

1. **Initial collection of evidence:** The school leader collects readily available data related to key aspects of school operation including policies, programs, reports, evaluation, demographics, and so on.

2. **Appointment of a data-analysis team:** An existing instructional leadership team may gather and analyze data, or a special data-analysis team could form. In this chapter, when you see the term data-analysis team, feel free to substitute instructional leadership team if you use that group to gather data. The team should be

small, consisting of six to eight voluntary members. A team could consist of the following members.

- Principal
- Instructional coach
- Math teacher
- Language arts teacher
- Special education teacher
- District representative, such as an assessment coordinator
- EL teacher
- Others as needed

3. **Investigation:** Investigation is the process in which the data-analysis team looks for specific evidence related to the operation of the school. These data build on the foundational work completed in the first step of the process where the school leader gathers operational data.

4. **Analysis of the evidence:** Once the data are gathered, the team analyzes them. During this analysis, the team looks for trends, anticipated findings, and unexpected findings. It is during this part of the process that the team condenses raw data into a manageable form that the team can then share and discuss with the larger school community.

5. **Schoolwide consensus building:** Once the team has analyzed and condensed the data, it is now ready for review by the entire school community. The instructional leadership or data team should present its findings to the staff and get their feedback.

6. **Selection and implementation of research-based school-improvement strategies:** In the final planning stage, Barr and Yates (2010) propose that the school community, in conjunction with the data-analysis or instructional leadership team, generate specific, research-proven strategies for the school-improvement process. In this step, the planning goes beyond the goals the community has identified in the previous step to identify specific strategies, ways to measure effectiveness of the implementation, and other planning features. Leaders can then share the plan with members of the school community not previously involved in the

planning and with school district officials (in conjunction with seeking their support, which we cover in detail in chapter 6).

Forming a Data-Analysis Team

When organizing a data-analysis team (or using an instructional leadership team to gather data), keep the following considerations in mind.

- ▸ **The role of the team:** Clearly communicating the team's role at the onset of the process will help you avoid misunderstandings and misperceptions. The team's purpose might be to analyze data and then report the information to you, to other stakeholders, or directly to the staff.

- ▸ **The scope of the work:** The scope of the team's work should also be clear. Will the team act in an advisory manner, or will it serve to develop the school-improvement plan? Will the team be involved through the development of the school-improvement plan, or will its recommendations be handed off to another decision-making entity?

- ▸ **Duration of team operations:** Be clear about how often and how long you plan to have the team work. Understanding the duration of team operations will help team members decide their level of commitment to the process. If the team will be meeting each week for two months, it may be easier for people to commit to it than if it's going to meet each week for the entire year. Also, identifying the duration of team operations can help team members develop the sense of urgency needed to get to work on the assigned tasks.

- ▸ **Characteristics of team members:** When choosing team members, consider their characteristics, such as their work, thinking, and processing styles. Choose a balance of informal leaders and those who like to follow, people who think globally versus those who think in a step-by-step manner, introspective thinkers versus those who process out loud, and senior staff members versus less experienced staff.

Figure 5.1 provides a worksheet for forming a data-analysis team.

Directions: A school data-analysis team is an important structure to have in place to gather and analyze data and potentially assist in the development of the school-improvement plan. Use this worksheet to help guide your development of this team.

1. **The role of the team:** What role will the team serve in the school? Will the team serve as representatives of the rest of the faculty? Will the team gather input from the other stakeholders? Will the team be the primary source of information for the stakeholders, or will there be a schoolwide strategy for disseminating information?

2. **The scope of the work:** Will the team act in an advisory manner, or will it serve to develop the school-improvement plan? Will the team be involved in the process through the development of the school-improvement plan, or will its recommendations be handed off to another decision-making entity?

3. **Duration of team operations:** How long will the team be in operation? How often will the team meet? What are some of the outcomes this team needs to reach before it completes its work?

4. **Characteristics of team members:** What kinds of work styles and processing styles must be present on this team? What would be the best mix of characteristics (years of experience, content-area expertise, number of years in the building, and so on) to help the team think outside of the box and objectively without compromising its success?

5. **Additional considerations:** What other considerations should you take into account in forming this team?

Figure 5.1: Guiding the formation of a school data-analysis team.

*Visit **go.SolutionTree.com/schoolimprovement** for a free reproducible version of this figure.*

Let's see how Charlotte Taylor, an elementary principal working to turn her school around, uses these principles to guide her selection of members of her school data-analysis team.

> Principal Charlotte Taylor prepares to organize a data-analysis team to gather and review data related to the school's performance. As she ponders forming the team, she reflects on the various personalities and styles she needs on the team.
>
> Principal Taylor wants a balance of leaders and followers to help avoid power struggles within the team. She wants some team members who are able to look at the big picture and at how all the data interact. But some team members should be detail-oriented, she thinks, to ensure that seemingly unimportant data will be considered in the analysis as well.
>
> Principal Taylor will include some team members who have been at the building more than five years to assist the rest of the team in understanding and appreciating the context of the data. Newer team members will also be important to include to ensure team members look at the data with fresh eyes.
>
> Team members from various academic areas in the school will be essential to ensure that data and ultimately the school-improvement plan reflect how all areas can be represented and contribute to the plan.
>
> Principal Taylor uses these criteria to determine which staff members to approach about serving on the school data-analysis team. Before long, a solid team emerges, and Principal Taylor is feeling optimistic about moving ahead with data gathering.

Principal Taylor was purposeful in populating her data-analysis team with diverse members with different processing and personality styles. This will provide multiple perspectives leading to more thorough data analysis. While working with a diverse team is helpful for data analysis, it can be challenging when conflicts arise as a result of the different personalities. It's important to provide teams with support and professional development to maximize their abilities to work together and positively resolve conflicts.

Tools for Team Success

For a data-analysis team to be successful, members need support. It is best to provide support from the beginning, rather than waiting for issues to arise and then providing the necessary support.

In the following sections, we describe tools and various support structures leaders can implement to increase the probability of success for a data-analysis team.

First Team Meeting Agenda

In your first meeting with the team, create an agenda that covers the team's purpose, role, and a timeline for the team's work. Share the guidelines for committee work (such as using objectivity, observing confidentiality, following team norms, and obtaining consensus). Share communication strategies that team members might keep in mind as they work together. Be sure to answer questions from team members and allow them to share any comments or concerns about the expectations.

Figure 5.2 shows a completed worksheet for creating an agenda for the first data-analysis team meeting.

Directions: Use the following worksheet to plan the agenda for the organizational meeting of the data-analysis team.

- **The purpose, role, and timeline for the team's work:** What topics will you present and discuss in the meeting?

Share with team members the purpose for the team is to gather data about all aspects of the school. The role of the team members is to serve as representatives of the entire faculty to objectively gather and analyze data. The team will meet twice each week for eight weeks.

- **Data-gathering plan and timeline:** How will the team work together? What will members be expected to focus on? What is the desired outcome for the work?

Share an outline of the plan using PowerPoint. Let team members know that during the first three weeks, the team may be subdivided into smaller workgroups with specific content-area responsibilities. Each small group will present the data it has gathered during the fourth week. During the fifth through eighth weeks, the entire team will analyze the data and come up with recommendations for the school-improvement plan.

- **Guidelines for the committee work:** What guidelines should team members follow as they work together?

Stress the need to be objective and remain neutral when gathering and analyzing the data—Define the term objectivity and provide examples where team members examined data with and without objectivity.

Stress the importance of appropriate confidentiality—Explain that team members should only share information with the entire faculty once the whole team has processed it.

Share the importance of following team ground rules or norms—Clarify the concept of ground rules and norms. Ask team members to meet in small groups to discuss the parameters or norms they feel they need in order to work together effectively. Have them complete an activity to outline those norms and those that are expected of them by leadership.

Figure 5.2: Completed worksheet for planning the first organizational data-analysis team meeting.

continued →

- **Communication strategies:** What communication strategies should the team use to facilitate their work together?

Share ideas related to two-way communication—Provide examples of listening and sharing as two-way communication strategies. Let the group discuss how members plan to gather information and share information with the groups they represent.

Share ideas related to consensus—What is it? How do we use it? Share a definition of consensus. Share the advantages of using consensus rather than voting.

- **Comments and questions:** Open up the meeting for any questions or comments from team members.

*Visit **go.SolutionTree.com/schoolimprovement** for a free reproducible version of this figure.*

Behavior Parameters

For data-analysis teams to be successful, the group needs to set behavior guidelines for its members. For teams, there are two basic kinds of behavior limits: ground rules and norms. Let's take a look at the similarities and differences of these two kinds of behavior limits.

1. **Ground rules:** Ground rules are behavior limits set by the group leader or facilitator. Leaders can set ground rules quickly to provide the guidelines. Ground rules work best for teams that lack the capacity to hold dialogue to set their own behavior limits. The major disadvantage with ground rules is that since the team is not involved in setting them, members are less likely to follow them.

2. **Norms:** Norms are the behavior limits that team members set for themselves. Since team members create their own norms, they are more committed to following them than they are to ground rules. Norms work best for teams that have the capacity to set their own behavior limits and build the long-term commitment to working together as a group. A disadvantage of norms is that they take time and dialogue to identify and set.

Following are some examples of norms and ground rules that guide teams to success.

- Come to team meetings ready to learn and make progress toward our goals.

- Leave negative emotions at the door when the team meets.

- Presume that all group members are trying to do their best during team meetings.

- Come to meetings with an open mind, ready to try new things and learn from others.

- ▸ Use active listening strategies while members share ideas, ask questions, or make suggestions.

- ▸ Try to understand other group members' perspectives on issues.

- ▸ During brainstorming activities, listen carefully and do not evaluate contributions until you've heard all ideas.

- ▸ Practice suspending your opinion temporarily when you initially hear an idea that is different than your perspective.

- ▸ Make sure that everyone has an equal chance to participate in conversations and dialogue.

- ▸ When a team member shares a new idea, do not agree or disagree too quickly.

- ▸ Honor time limits and commitments.

- ▸ Look at the pros and cons of an issue before making a final decision.

- ▸ Work to preserve the equal status of all members on this team.

- ▸ Understand and mediate the influence you and your comments have on others in this group.

- ▸ Try to get more details about an idea or issue before making a final decision.

- ▸ Use reflective paraphrases to help other team members know that you understand the points they are making.

- ▸ If you do not understand a suggestion or the information another team member has communicated, ask clarifying questions to gain more information.

- ▸ Use clarifying questions that are open ended and nonjudgmental.

- ▸ Follow the group-determined guidelines when communicating with those not on this committee.

All of the norms and ground rules in the list are positively stated. Team members respond more favorably to descriptions of what they *should do* rather than what they *shouldn't do*. You'll also notice that most of the norms and ground rules are somewhat generic. Some teams find it beneficial to personalize their norms. For example, a generic norm is "use active listening strategies while members share ideas, ask questions, or make suggestions." The personalized version is "we will use active listening strategies while team members share ideas, ask questions, or make suggestions." By making norms more focused on what *we* will do, they take on more meaning for team members.

The worksheet in figure 5.3 will help you determine whether to provide ground rules or involve your data-analysis team in setting their own norms.

Directions: There are certain team characteristics that can help determine whether the leader sets ground rules or asks the team to set its own norms for meeting behavior parameters.

Rate your data-analysis team using the following list of characteristics. After you have rated each characteristic, add your scores to determine which behavior parameter strategy—norms or ground rules—best fits your team's strengths and needs.

	Level
1. Team members' ability to have an honest dialogue about their present level of effectiveness and their behavior parameter needs	1 2 3 4 5 1 = Low and 5 = High
2. Number of people in the group who have strong personalities or want to "run the team"	1 2 3 4 5 1 = High and 5 = Low
3. Amount of issues or baggage present from past work experiences with one another	1 2 3 4 5 1 = High and 5 = Low
4. Amount of importance team places on having behavior parameters	1 2 3 4 5 1 = Low and 5 = High
5. Level of leadership (external) or principal control the team is accustomed to having (lack of team autonomy)	1 2 3 4 5 1 = High and 5 = Low
6. Level of confidence and self-directedness of the team members	1 2 3 4 5 1 = Low and 5 = High
7. Level of competence and confidence of the team leader	1 2 3 4 5 1 = Low and 5 = High
8. Team's commitment to accomplishing the task	1 2 3 4 5 1 = Low and 5 = High

Total _____

The higher the total number, the more likely the team will benefit from operating with norms. The lower the total number, the more likely the team may need ground rules.

While this assessment can give you a good indication about your team's capacity to use norms or ground rules, use your judgment and common sense in addition to the numbers to make your final decision. Also, some teams may need ground rules to start the process but increase their operating effectiveness in order to move toward norms.

Figure 5.3: Worksheet for using norms versus ground rules.

*Visit **go.SolutionTree.com/schoolimprovement** for a free reproducible version of this figure.*

For teams that might be better suited to setting their own operating norms, try leading the following seven-step activity.

1. Gather the data-analysis team members to discuss the importance of clear operating norms.

2. Divide the team into smaller pair or trio groups.

3. Ask each smaller group to respond to the following questions on chart paper.

   As we work together . . .

   - What kinds of support or structures do we expect from our team leader for our team to be successful?

   - What behaviors do we expect from one another as data-analysis team members in order to make the team successful?

   - What behaviors should we expect from ourselves as individuals for our data-analysis team to be successful?

4. Once all the groups have completed their lists, ask each one to report their work to the larger group.

5. Ask other group members to summarize the common elements in the lists.

6. Once the team members have identified the common aspects, ask them to select the norms they can agree to follow.

7. Combine the agreed-upon norms into one document to share with team members.

This activity provides the structure some data-analysis teams need to set norms that everyone can agree to and follow as they work together.

Communication Skills

For data-analysis teams to function effectively, members need to communicate effectively. Some of the more important communication skills include listening, paraphrasing and reflecting, open-ended questioning, summarizing, and other communication skills that help team members feel understood and valued. Even though team members might communicate well with students in their classrooms, these communication skills don't always transfer to situations involving work with other adults.

Two-Way Communication Strategies

Two-way communication strategies are methods data-analysis team members use to gather input from their colleagues and share information back with them once the team has made some preliminary decisions.

Depending on the role of the team in the school-improvement planning process, gathering input may be more important than sharing information. Gathering input may not be a skill with which data-analysis team members have extensive experience, so some focused training may be needed. Some data-gathering activities could include talking to teachers about their classroom data and asking teachers about the recent results on their formative and summative assessments. The team then shares the data they gathered with the faculty at a staff meeting.

Skills to Minimize Conflict

One of the biggest obstacles to team success is conflict. The emotions triggered by the failing school identification coupled with differences of opinion and lack of experience working collaboratively outside of the classroom can provide fertile ground for conflict.

The development of ground rules or norms and organized meeting structures can help to minimize conflict, but effective leaders take a proactive stance in helping teams to deal with conflict before it becomes a problem. Let's return to Principal Charlotte Taylor's school to see how her team deals productively with conflict.

After Principal Charlotte Taylor forms her data-analysis team, she reviews the characteristics of team members to determine what training the team will require. One area in which they would benefit from training is in dealing with conflict. She decides to use an activity to help team members get to know one another and understand how they might process information and communicate in different ways.

Principal Taylor starts off the professional development session by telling team members why she desires a team comprised of individuals with diverse processing and communication styles. Next, the team participates in an activity to identify their preferred processing styles, the strengths and limitations of these styles, and strategies to work successfully with team members who have different styles. Team members enjoy the activity, and several members mention how helpful the information would be for use outside the team as well, in working with colleagues, students, and in situations outside of school. They even recommend that Principal Taylor consider implementing the activity with the entire staff.

Once team members complete the activity, Principal Taylor asks them to develop their team meeting norms and operating procedures. They also discuss how they plan to handle conflict situations that arise within the team.

In this example, we see how Principal Taylor took a proactive stance in dealing with issues that could potentially negatively impact or derail the operation of the team. By providing team members with information about the various processing styles, then helping them to discuss how they could address issues that may come up, Principal Taylor increased the probability of success for the diverse team.

Meeting Structures

Since the work of data-analysis teams can be time-consuming and complex, leaders should ensure that team meeting time is as productive as possible. Efficient meetings require members to develop and follow an agenda.

Agendas act as frames to hold the meeting content together. When a group attends a meeting with a well-developed agenda, members know what to expect and can plan their thought processes to match the major topics of conversation planned for the meeting.

The following considerations will help ensure the meeting agenda (developed by the principal in collaboration with the team leader) will maximize team members' use of time and energy.

- Schedule the most important topics early in the meeting.

- Think about the amount of time needed for each agenda item. Do not overload the agenda with too many items.

- Designate the appropriate amount of time needed for each agenda item. Identify a timekeeper to keep the meeting on track.

- Avoid one person (usually a team leader) managing all of the agenda items. Delegating responsibility for some agenda items to team members builds commitment and ensures team member engagement.

- Let team members know the process or outcomes for each agenda item. If an item requires a decision at the end of a conversation, label it appropriately on the agenda. If an item is intended to be informational in nature, team members should know that as well. Labeling the process or outcomes for agenda items helps team members prepare appropriately.

Figure 5.4 (page 98) is a sample completed agenda template utilizing the components of an effective meeting structure. Note that in the example,

Data-Analysis Team Meeting: October 4

Agenda Item	Time Needed	Resources Needed	Process or Outcome of the Item	Follow-Up
1. Share good news (team leader facilitates).	Five minutes	None	To learn about some of the positive things happening at the school	Team will share more ideas at future meetings.
2. Report of data-gathering process (each subcommittee reports)	Thirty minutes	Handouts detailing planned versus actual process	Informational: To learn about each subcommittee's process Problem solving: To share strategies for teams experiencing difficulty in finding data	Subcommittees report on new progress at the next meeting.
3. Discussion of the process for conducting the school community meeting (the meeting subcommittee report and findings)	Twenty minutes	Handouts containing the possible meeting agenda	Informational: To inform the data-analysis team about the next steps in the process Decision making: To have the data-analysis team make decisions about the agenda so arrangements can be made to hold the meeting	A subcommittee will make the needed arrangements to hold the school community informational meeting.
4. Summarize the progress in the meeting; discuss and plan the agenda of the next meeting (team leader facilitates).	Five minutes	The meeting agenda planning template	Discussion and decision: To help the data-analysis team prioritize the agenda items to have a productive meeting	Team leader sends out finalized agenda one day before the next meeting.

Figure 5.4: Template and sample completed team agenda.

*Visit **go.SolutionTree.com/schoolimprovement** for a free reproducible version of this figure.*

details are brief but provide enough information that participants can see the major elements of the meeting and some of the rationale for these elements. Column four contains processes and outcomes for each meeting agenda. This helps team members understand the goal of each agenda item.

Now that the data-analysis team is formed and trained for their work, it's time for the team to begin its work gathering data.

Starting the Data-Gathering Process

Schools have extensive data at their disposal. The focus of the data-analysis team will depend on the challenges the school is facing. Here are some common sources of data from which school teams may gather.

- Policies and procedures that may impact students, such as the attendance policy, tardy policy, the suspension policy, and others
- Course and program offerings
- The time allotted for each academic content area or course
- Standardized testing scores
- Local assessment results
- Grading practices and trends in student grades
- Formative and summative assessment results
- Districtwide benchmarks
- The number of students receiving interventions
- Parent-teacher conference attendance rates
- Unpacking the academic standards
- Attendance records
- Office referral rates

These types of data are primarily quantitative or numerical. With quantitative data, teams look for averages, trends, and frequencies. They provide measurable information about core elements of school performance and student learning.

Quantitative Data

The data-analysis team's first focus will likely be on gathering quantitative data. Barr and Yates (2010) provide a map to help teams identify key data sets identified by the Maryland State Department of Education (2011) and where they may be located. This map appears in figure 5.5 (pages 100–103).

A majority of the data in Barr and Yates's (2010) map is quantitative or numerical. While quantitative data are important and provide a good foundation for the development of a school-improvement plan, there are other data that school leaders and data teams will find helpful.

Type of Data	Where Data May Be Located				Status	
	State Department of Education	Central Office	School	Other*	Data Collected	Data Unavailable
Student Demographics and School Information						
Total enrollment	✓	✓				
Grade-level enrollment	✓	✓				
Subgroups (number of students in each)	✓	✓				
Mobility percentage (entrants and withdrawals)	✓	✓				
Attendance percentage	✓	✓				
Expulsion number	✓	✓				
Suspension number	✓	✓				
Dropout rate	✓	✓				
Graduation rate	✓	✓				
High school diploma rate	✓	✓				
Staff Profile						
Principal (length of time at the school, years of experience, certificates)		✓	✓			
Number of assistant principals, other administrators, and their assignments		✓	✓			
Number and percentage of teaching faculty's total classroom instructional experience		✓	✓			
Number and percentage of teaching faculty's service at this school		✓	✓			
Number and percentage of classes not taught by highly qualified teachers	✓	✓				

Type of Data	Where Data May Be Located				Status	
	State Department of Education	Central Office	School	Other*	Data Collected	Data Unavailable
Total number of teachers		✓	✓			
Number of school-based reading and English teachers		✓	✓			
Number of school-based mathematics and algebra or data-analysis teachers		✓	✓			
Number of school-based reading and English resource personnel		✓	✓			
Number of school-based mathematics and algebra or data-analysis resource personnel		✓	✓			
Number of paraprofessionals who are highly qualified		✓	✓			
Number of paraprofessionals who are yet to be highly qualified		✓	✓			
Teacher and administrator attendance		✓	✓			
Student Achievement Data						
Adequate yearly progress (AYP) for reading and English	✓					
AYP for mathematics and algebra or data analysis	✓					
Subgroup data by content, grade level, subscores, and by number and percentage at advanced, proficient, and basic	✓					

Figure 5.5: Data-gathering map.

continued →

Type of Data	Where Data May Be Located				Status	
	State Department of Education	Central Office	School	Other*	Data Collected	Data Unavailable
Subgroup data by confidence interval	✓					
School-improvement status	✓	✓	✓			
Title I Data						
School choice (transfers out)	✓					
Supplemental educational services	✓					
Schoolwide and targeted assistance programs		✓	✓			
English Learners Data						
English language proficiency tests		✓	✓			
Annual measurable achievement objectives		✓	✓			
Language and cultural background data		✓	✓			
Special Education Data						
Number and types of disabilities	✓	✓				
Disproportionality data	✓	✓				
Least restrictive environment data	✓	✓				
Summary of compliance results	✓	✓				
Instructional Data						
Instructional goals and objectives		✓	✓			
Core reading and English programs		✓	✓			
Core mathematics and algebra or data-analysis programs		✓	✓			
Reading and English intervention programs		✓	✓			
Mathematics and algebra or data-analysis intervention programs		✓	✓			

Type of Data	Where Data May Be Located				Status	
	State Department of Education	Central Office	School	Other*	Data Collected	Data Unavailable
Enrichment, extended day, and summer programs (number of students, target population, content focus, length of time, grade levels, attendance, and so on)		✓	✓			
School- and District-Level Data						
School board policies regarding instruction, curriculum, parents and families, assessment, and so on		✓	✓			
School operating budget		✓	✓			
Partnerships (with whom, for what purpose, and so on)		✓	✓			
School scheduling		✓	✓			
Pilot projects		✓	✓			
Grants (title, purpose, amount, target audience, and so on)		✓	✓			
Professional development topics, scheduling, attendance, and so on		✓	✓			
Gifted and Talented Data						
Community Demographic Data: Income, Unemployment, Minority Make-Up, and So On						

Note: *For example, websites, community databases, and so on

Source: Barr & Yates, 2010, pp. 161–164. School improvement data sets from Maryland State Department of Education, 2011.

*Visit **go.SolutionTree.com/schoolimprovement** for a free reproducible version of this figure.*

Qualitative Data

Qualitative data are more verbal and descriptive in nature, important but not measurable in a precise way. Some qualitative data sources school leaders and data-analysis teams might use include the following.

▸ Interview summaries (from interviews with students, faculty and staff, parents, and community members)

▸ Focus group summaries (from meetings of stakeholders in which they respond to questions as a whole group)

▸ Information from surveys and questionnaires (administered online or on paper showing the perceptions of major stakeholders)

▸ Anecdotal reviews (from written descriptions of major school operations, policies, and so on, by stakeholder groups)

▸ Policy, procedure, and rule analysis (of major written information guiding the school)

▸ Analysis of artifacts (information related to posted items, signs, student work, school mission or motto, and other displayed items at the school gathered by groups such as the school instructional leadership team, collaborative teams, and other groups in the school)

▸ Analysis of community and parent involvement programs (assessments of the purposes, impact of, and participation in parent and community involvement programs)

In examining verbal or qualitative data, the school leader and data-analysis team have to review the information and infer trends and make generalizations. For example, a data team may review comments by parents on an open-ended questionnaire. In looking at the comments, they may find there are some common answers for what parents like about the school or what they think needs improvement. By reviewing and discussing these comments, they identify trends they can use in their analysis of the school.

The last data source on the previous list is the analysis of community and parent involvement programs. Analyzing these programs to determine their interest and impact can be helpful to a leader and a data-analysis team that is working to flip a school. If parent programs are not meeting their intended purposes or if there is minimal interest in these programs, the principal and the school instructional leadership team should re-evaluate these activities and consider reallocating the resources dedicated to them to other, more productive programs that have the ability to assist the school in its turnaround effort. Figure 5.6 shows a template for gathering and organizing data related to these programs. Using the template, teams gather data related to the following three areas of program implementation.

1. **Programs for school–community participation:** Schools typically implement programs through which the community can engage with the school. The programs that may fit into this category include volunteer programs, events open to the community, programs where students volunteer in the community, and so on.

2. **School–community partnerships:** Examples include school and local business partnerships, partnerships with churches, the parent organization, and others that make sense for both the school and the partner organization.

3. **Parent participation activites:** Schools typically offer programming that encourages parents to become involved in their child's education. Examples of these programs include parent-teacher conferences, family academic events (for example, family math night), extracurricular presentations and programs, and so on.

1. Programs for School-Community Participation		
Program Name	**Program Intent**	**Actual Impact (hours, products, and so on)**
Report and analysis of information:		

2. School-Community Partnerships			
Program Name	**Partner Name**	**Program Intent**	**Actual Impact**
Report and analysis of information:			

3. Parent Participation Activities (conferences, drama programs, curriculum nights, and so on)		
Program	**Program Intent**	**Participation Rate**
Report and analysis of information:		

Figure 5.6: Assessing school and community programs worksheet.

*Visit **go.SolutionTree.com/schoolimprovement** for a free reproducible version of this figure.*

Since the data that teams gather for the form in figure 5.6 are qualitative or descriptive in nature, teams must carefully review them when looking for trends and general themes to draw conclusions about the programs. It is helpful for leaders and data teams to consider how to combine this descriptive information with more quantitative or numerical data to assess the impact of programs. For example, let's say that the quantitative data show that the rate of parents attending parental involvement sessions is low. Team members may want to look at the intended purposes of parental participation sessions to see if the sessions are actually accomplishing their purposes. Let's see how this concept plays out in the following example.

> The data-analysis team at Spence High School is preparing to schedule a major parental-involvement event where parents will meet as a large group to discuss general information about the school, the methods teachers use to communicate with them, and other aspects of school operation. This event is typically scheduled for two hours on a weekend and takes a lot of preparation and planning to make it successful. Over the years, attendance at this meeting has been dwindling.

> In completing the assessment in figure 5.6 (page 105), the data-analysis team finds that the purpose of the meeting and parental needs related to the meeting have changed. When the program was started, parents had limited information about the school, so they attended the meeting. In recent years, teachers reach out to parents before the start of the school year to provide information and answer questions. Thus, there is less need for the group session. The school website has been restructured, so that many of the questions and concerns parents express at the meeting are now addressed online where parents can easily access the information. After completing the analysis of the program, the team finds that it no longer serves the functions it had been designed for in its initial implementation.

> The data-analysis team shares its findings with Principal Julie Morris. After reviewing the quantitative data showing reduced parental attendance and the qualitative review of the parental programs using the template in figure 5.6, the team and Principal Morris recommend eliminating the program, which allows energy and resources to be redirected into programs with current relevance.

In this example, we see how the data-analysis team worked with Principal Morris to combine qualitative and quantitative data to assess the effectiveness of one of the school programs. Because human resources and budgetary resources are finite, it's important that every program makes a maximum contribution to the school and its improvement goals.

Assessing School Culture

As the previous section shows, a variety of important data may not be available or best expressed in quantitative form. Teams need to be certain to give descriptive or qualitative data-collection methods adequate attention. One area that is rich with qualitative data is school culture.

Edgar Schein (2016), who is often referred to as the father of organizational culture, provides a clear structure for the examination of organizational culture. He identifies three levels of culture: (1) artifacts, (2) espoused beliefs and values, and (3) basic underlying assumptions. We further discuss the concept of organizational and school culture in chapter 7 (page 133). Here, we briefly examine Schein's (2016) three levels as they pertain to school culture, and provide examples of how a data-analysis team might assess these three levels.

Artifacts

Artifacts are visible or observable products, processes, or behaviors that indicate the core beliefs and operations of the school. For example, in a culture that is focused on student success, a person visiting the school might see examples of student accomplishments posted on the walls, after-school academic clubs in operation, collaborative grade-level teams meeting to keep students on track with expected learning, and other observable products or processes. Most artifacts can be measured by gathering them and then drawing conclusions based on the findings.

Espoused Beliefs and Values

Espoused beliefs and values are elements that are embedded in the minds of those in the school and used to guide decision making. For example, if those in the school community believe that all students can learn, then conversations with teachers who are working with struggling students should reveal a can-do attitude. Teachers do not give up on students easily. They are engaged with collaborative teams to look for ways to reach struggling students. Data-analysis teams can assess espoused beliefs and values by talking to collaborative team members throughout the school and listening to what they say compared to what they *do*. Also, there should be artifacts that are congruent to what people *say* they value. The lack of congruence in some situations could indicate a problem with the culture. For example, if the motto of the school is "every student, every day" but teachers remove disruptive students immediately from their classrooms, their espoused beliefs don't match their actions. This could indicate a problem in the school's culture.

Basic Underlying Assumptions

On a deeper level that contains espoused beliefs and values, basic underlying assumptions are so ingrained in the minds of school community members that they guide actions in an almost automatic way. For example, if a school community really believes one of its core cultural values is providing success for all students, team members will naturally work together to problem solve a student learning situation as their first response rather than becoming frustrated and looking for excuses for why the situation won't work. Teams can assess basic underlying assumptions by talking with school community members to gain examples of how they approach situations.

Let's see how a principal, Hersha Grant, uses the three levels of culture to assess the culture of her school.

Hersha Grant, a high school principal, is in the process of gathering data related to the culture of her school. She uses the work of Schein (2016) to inform her data-gathering and examination process. She focuses on artifacts, espoused values and beliefs, and basic underlying assumptions.

She spends one day (as she conducts classroom walkthroughs) observing some of the artifacts visible in the school. She makes note of what she sees in the halls, of how organized and clean the school is, of what she sees on the walls and boards in the classrooms, and what she hears teachers say as they work with their students. She notes information in the teacher work rooms. She is vigilant to all other aspects she notices as she walks around the school.

Principal Grant uses the following chart to gather this information (figure 5.7).

When Principal Grant returns to her office, she spends an hour classifying the data she gathered into two groups: positive artifacts and negative artifacts. She then examines the artifacts and classifies them again using the following process (figure 5.8).

Observed Artifacts: Walkthrough, October 1	
Artifact Description	**Artifact Details**
• College posters and pennants	• These are posted at all classroom entrances.
• Classroom activities	• Teachers start classes with an activity while they handle management duties.
• Hallway posters	• There are mostly sports posters in the halls. Posters feature very few other extracurricular activities. • Posters are in English even though multiple languages are spoken.
• Student movement	• Teachers go to doorways to greet and dismiss students. There is orderly movement.

Figure 5.7: Observed artifacts.

Observed Artifacts: Walkthrough, October 1	
Observed Artifacts That Promote a Culture of Supporting Students and Learning	**Observed Artifacts That Do Not Promote a Culture of Supporting Students and Learning**
• Teachers monitored the classroom to maintain a safe, orderly learning environment. • Examples of student work (both exemplary and work involving effort) were posted. • Most teachers had a learning activity in place when the students entered the classroom.	• A small number of teachers were not standing in the halls during passing time. • The lack of diversity in the type of activities featured on posters does not recognize the value of other extra-curricular activities. • Only featuring posters in English may make some students feel unwelcome.

Figure 5.8: Observed artifacts classified into those that support the culture and those that do not.

Principal Grant notices after her initial classification of the artifacts that most of them are positive and promote the school's focus on student success. In her continued examination of the culture, she decides to conduct interviews to gather staff members' thoughts related to espoused values and underlying assumptions.

In the example, Principal Grant gathered descriptive or qualitative data related to several core attributes that provide a picture of the culture of the school. She will gather even more descriptive or qualitative data as she focuses on deeper aspects related to the culture. Once she has completed her examination of the three cultural aspects, she can then decide whether or not the school culture requires intervention to improve it or reinforcement to keep it moving in the right direction.

Let's look at another example of a school culture. The data in this example reveal a school that needs to focus on building school culture if it is to be successful in the turnaround process.

> John Garcia, an education consultant, is visiting a school to assist its leadership team in a turnaround effort. As Dr. Garcia approaches the school, he notices that it isn't well kept; the grass is long and the shrubbery overgrown. A parent volunteer greets Dr. Garcia at the front door and then leaves him there unattended to go to the office to notify staff of his arrival. The parent volunteer returns a few minutes later to escort Dr. Garcia to the office.
>
> Once in, Dr. Garcia immediately feels the chaos. Several students and parents are walking around the office, talking and waiting to speak with a staff member. It is apparent there is no system for dealing with visitors. When Dr. Garcia is finally able to talk with the principal, they are constantly interrupted by parents and teachers with problems they want to discuss with the principal.
>
> As Dr. Garcia walks through the school with one of the assistant principals, he notices that few teachers are in the halls during class transitions. In classrooms, the teachers have students working in groups, but most of their teaching is from the front of the room behind computer tables. There is very little monitoring of student learning occurring during the lessons.
>
> While moving from class to class, Dr. Garcia notices that the halls are not in order. There are papers on the floors, and very little student work or other materials appear on the walls.
>
> Finally, Dr. Garcia visits the teachers' workroom. In the workroom, teachers type silently on their laptops, planning their lessons. There is little interaction between them. Dr. Garcia's conversations with the teachers reveal that they don't have regular staff meetings, and when they do meet, the content is usually informational in the form of announcements. They express that they have little opportunity for discussion, sharing ideas, or working together.

In this brief example, we see a school that is quite different than the example we examined earlier. While the school may have the necessary components to positively impact student learning, leadership and staff seem disconnected and unorganized. The artifacts Dr. Garcia observed lead him to the conclusion that there is a lack of cohesive school culture present. If the turnaround process is to be successful, the school leader and staff will have to focus on culture building.

Tools for Assessing School Culture

Consider the form in figure 5.9 to use in gathering data related to school culture.

Directions: Use the following form to make note of and track the results of your school culture examination. After examining each aspect of school culture, use the data to identify any themes or generalizations that emerge.

Date of examination: _____

Person examining the elements: _____

Data Related to Observable Artifacts

Use this section to keep track of the various artifacts you observe as you walk through the building or classrooms.

Artifact Description	Artifact Details

Data Related to Espoused Beliefs and Values

Use this section to gather information from interviews, discussions, and observed behaviors that point to people's espoused beliefs and values.

Interview Comments, Discussion Details, and Observed Behaviors	Relationship Between Comments, Details, and Actions and School Culture Element

Data Related to Basic Underlying Assumptions

Use this section to keep track of comments, details, and actions that help you pinpoint or identify some of the basic aspects of school culture.

Interview Comments, Discussion Details, and Observed Behaviors	Relationship Between Comments, Details, and Actions and School Culture Element

---

Figure 5.9: Form for gathering initial school culture data.

*Visit **go.SolutionTree.com/schoolimprovement** for a free reproducible version of this figure.*

Another source that data teams and school leaders would be wise to tap for turnaround is parents. Their perceptions and opinions can shed valuable light on conditions in the school.

Gathering and Assessing Data From Parents

When gathering data from parents, consider using methods that will maximize the ease of sharing information with comfort and convenience. Some data-gathering methods we recommend include parent surveys, parent interviews, and parent focus groups.

Parent Surveys

A common method to quickly gather parental-perception data is with a survey, either pencil and paper or electronic. Surveys are highly efficient. Data-analysis teams can quickly compile and analyze the data from surveys. The school leader and data-analysis team can write surveys to gather the data they need to understand important parent perspectives about the school. Keep the following points in mind as you develop and implement surveys for gathering parental feedback.

- **Keep the survey brief and concise:** Be short and to the point to help minimize the time you are asking parents to devote to the survey.

- **Keep questions targeted:** Make sure survey questions will elicit the necessary information required for your school-improvement goals.

- **Keep questions focused on areas in which parents have knowledge:** For example, asking parents about their children's perceptions of school might be more fruitful than asking them specific information about how to improve the teaching at the school.

- **Consider the resources parents have to complete a survey:** If using an electronic survey, keep in mind that some parents may not have access to the internet at home. You may want to provide them with opportunities to complete the survey using the school's computers. Consider translating surveys into parents' home language. Send surveys home with students to bring back to school once completed.

- **Consider using existing opportunities for parents to complete surveys:** Some schools have paper copies of surveys available for parents to complete as they are waiting for parent-teacher conferences or other meetings. Schools could also include surveys inside programs or agendas for school-sponsored family events. Parents can complete them as they wait in the office area for appointments, and at other strategic opportunities.

While surveys can provide information from a larger group of parents, it's also helpful to gather more descriptive or qualitative data. There are a variety of ways to gather this type of information from parents, including individual interviews and focus groups.

Parent Interviews and Focus Group Information

Parent interviews and focus groups can be highly effective ways to gain specific, thorough, and in-depth information about parent perceptions of the school. The school principal, members from the data-analysis team, or others who can ask questions and remain neutral as parents answer them can conduct interviews and focus groups. It's a good idea to generate a pool of parents who represent multiple perspectives or experiences at the school. You may want to have parents who have had multiple children attend the school, parents of students who are relatively new to the school, parents from the cultural and ethnic groups that make up the school's population, and those who represent a variety of other backgrounds and perspectives. Interviews should last from fifteen to twenty minutes.

As you think about implementing parental interviews and focus groups, consider the following points.

▸ **If possible, make selection of interviewees and focus group participants random:** If selected parents are those known within the school (parent volunteers or others who are deeply involved in the school), the results of the survey could be tainted. It will be helpful to use a process such as drawing names from a box, selecting every fifth person from a list, and so on to select a random group. Once selections have been made, send parents an invitation to attend the interview or focus group.

▸ **Design a set of guiding questions for the interview or focus group in advance:** Use these guiding questions to make sure you stay on track and gain the important information you want to learn from parents.

▸ **Address parent needs during interviews and focus groups:** Consider providing resources to address parent needs when participating in interviews and focus groups at the school. For example, parents often need babysitting. Consider using local organizations such as Girl Scouts, National Honor Society, and others that seek opportunities for students to do service or volunteer projects. Provide food, interpreters to help with language issues, and other offerings that could help parents feel welcome and valued.

▸ **Take detailed notes or otherwise capture the information from each person:** One option is to record interviews, though some parents may be uncomfortable being recorded, so notify them of any plans to record at the start of the interview.

Chapter Summary

In the scenario we present at the beginning of this chapter, we see how Principal Miguel Martinez uses a systematic and thorough process to gather data from a variety of sources to inform the school-improvement plan. Let's see how this process helps Principal Martinez and his team as the year progresses.

As spring approaches, Principal Martinez and his instructional leadership team prepare for the monthly review of the school-improvement plan. Even though Principal Martinez and the team thought they did a thorough job looking at all available data sources at the beginning of the year, other pertinent data emerged as the year progressed. For example, the rate of parental engagement and involvement and the level of student engagement during instruction have become areas that the school-improvement team thinks might be negatively affecting student achievement. For this reason, the team decides to address these issues and integrate them into the existing goals in the school-improvement plan.

Before long, the instructional leadership team has good news to share: quarterly grade averages for students are improving. Also, teachers report that students are more engaged and involved in their classrooms. Student attendance has increased slightly and is going in the right direction. The turnaround is in motion.

In this scenario, we see how the extra time Principal Martinez spent with his team analyzing multiple data sources is paying off. By continuing to meet, collect, and analyze data, the team is able to revisit the school-improvement plan to evaluate its effectiveness. Subsequently, the team recognizes the school's progress and identifies additional strategies to keep the plan on track.

In this chapter, we examined the importance of gathering and analyzing data and how to do so to have an impact on school turnaround. In the next chapter, we explore how to match the school's needs with the support the school district can provide to make the school-turnaround process a success.

Reflection Questions

As you reflect on the content of this chapter, answer the following questions.

1. Why is it important to identify an instructional leadership team or data-analysis team to assist in gathering data related to student achievement and learning?

2. Why is it important to gather both qualitative and quantitative data in a school?

3. What are some strategies to successfully gather qualitative or descriptive data? How can a principal maximize the discussion during a focus-group session?

4. How can asking parents for their perceptions of the school in surveys, interviews, and focus groups help the data-analysis team and the principal identify areas of strength and needed improvements?

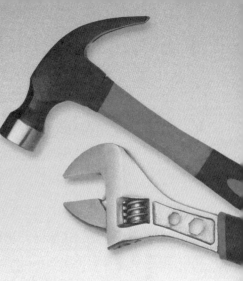

Chapter 6

Obtaining Commitment From the District

Shelley Newsome has been transferred to the principal position at Noles High School, a school in need of turnaround. She is excited for the opportunity, but she knows the position will require a lot of work—not just within the school building, but with district leadership as well. She knows that certain resources and support from the district will be necessary for successful turnaround.

Ms. Newsome schedules a meeting with the superintendent, Katherine Johnson, to discuss some of the resources and support she will need in turning around the school. When making the appointment for the meeting, Ms. Newsome lets Dr. Johnson's administrative assistant know she would like to discuss Dr. Johnson's thoughts and expectations for Noles High School plus some of the ways the school district plans to support the turnaround. While she is waiting for the meeting date, Principal Newsome brainstorms a list of needs to help guide her conversation with the superintendent.

At the beginning of the meeting, Superintendent Johnson shares how happy she is that Ms. Newsome will be the principal this fall at Noles High School. She also shares her confidence in Ms. Newsome and her vision for how she would like to see the school change along with several specific outcomes for both short-term and long-term goals.

Ms. Newsome takes careful notes during the conversation. She then asks if they can discuss her resource needs at Noles High School. Both Dr. Johnson and Ms. Newsome have several of the same ideas in mind, but they differ on a few.

For example, they both thought external content-area experts would be good to utilize as the teachers work to tie their teaching closer to the standards in their content areas. Ms. Newsome had listed for the school district to consider moving two negative staff members out of Noles. Superintendent Johnson said she'd like to think about the ripple effects of that strategy.

They decide to take some time to review one another's ideas and meet again to discuss them in a few days. This time will give both Ms. Newsome and Superintendent Johnson the chance to think about the goals and needs, plus add additional ideas they think will be helpful for the school.

In this brief example, we see how Ms. Newsome begins the process of negotiating some of the resources she will need to increase her chances of successful turnaround at Noles High School. Ms. Newsome understands that she will need to have access to certain district resources in order to have a chance at success. For example, utilizing district instructional coaching resources could help the teachers learn and implement new instructional skills. Working with the district curriculum leaders could help the teachers unpack the standards and align their teaching to them.

Even though leaders implement turnaround efforts at the school level, districts are instrumental in the success of such projects. School districts need to find the delicate balance between providing appropriate resources and support but not micromanaging the school-improvement process. The level of direct district intervention and the amount of autonomy the district will provide should be discussed at the start of the flipping or turnaround project. Having this discussion will let everyone know the expectations up front for the support and interaction. The principal of a turnaround school can help the school district define its support. Many school districts and principals forget this important part of the school-turnaround process and don't determine how the district will support the school.

In a report by the Center for American Progress summarizing some of the research related to improving failing schools, Tiffany D. Miller and Catherine Brown (2015) report that "the most compelling finding from this research review is that school turnaround is possible and that it occurs when districts take aggressive steps" (p. 7). School-improvement specialist Daniel L. Duke (2015) notes that "without capable and committed school district leadership, the hard work of principals may be for naught" (p. 199). If the superintendent and district office staff don't get involved in supporting the principal in the turnaround process, it becomes difficult to be successful.

In this chapter, we explore the role school districts play in the turnaround process, how to identify helpful school district support as you refine your school-improvement plan, and how to develop an outline for a meeting with the superintendent and district personnel to enlist their support and negotiate elements of your plan.

Engaging the District in the Turnaround Effort

The school district and superintendent can support turnaround principals in a variety of ways. Duke (2015) outlines several ways. We've clarified and added examples to Duke's original points in the following list. The original items from Duke's list appear in bold while our additions and examples follow each bold point.

- **Providing top-level leadership for turnaround initiatives:**
  - A dedicated central office person whose only assignment is to assist the school in the turnaround process
  - Focused and specialized professional development for leading turnaround efforts
  - Emotional support (a coach or other support person) for the principal to use as a sounding board (different from the dedicated central office person assisting in the turnaround process)
  - A liaison between the school board and the turnaround principal
  - Parent and police liaison services to build relationships with students and the community; for example, a school resource officer to increase the appearance of a safe learning environment and let students build relationships with the officer. Parent liaisons can represent the various parent groups or cultures in the schools. They can provide important information and perspectives for turnaround principals to use as they move forward in their turnaround effort.
- **Developing capable school leaders:**
  - Assistance in developing the turnaround plan
  - Extra professional development related to turnaround needs
- **Assisting with school staffing and faculty development:**
  - Extra staffing positions in key academic areas
  - Priority access to master teachers in the hiring pool and from other schools

- Incentives for teachers to want to work in the turnaround school
- Openness to moving extremely negative or resistant teachers and staff members to other schools to gain traction for successful turnaround
- Funding for cleaning, repairs, and extra staffing for building maintenance
- Counseling to teachers and staff as they work through difficult situations, conversations, and so on, during the turnaround process
- Content-area coaches and peer coaches to help teachers improve their instructional practices
- Facilitators to conduct meetings so the principal can participate in planning with the staff
- Access to dedicated time with district content experts
- Full-time substitutes and extra training and support for substitute teachers working in the turnaround school

▸ **Providing technical support and supplementary resources:**

- Access to district public relations resources to help manage information flow, produce internal communication tools, work with local media sources, manage social media resources, and so on
- Access to the school district's attorney for questions or legal advice and dealing with union issues that may arise in relation to the turnaround effort
- Help with administrative tasks so the turnaround principal can focus on the school-improvement process
- Translation services

▸ **Restructuring to facilitate district support services:**

- Differentiated funding to provide more resources for the school to raise academic achievement
- Additional funds to help with implementation of new programs
- Access to district administrative assistant time and resources
- Flexibility to restructure the day, change the schedule, change the building configuration, and so on to meet academic goals

▸ **Providing ample data:**

 ◆ Data for current student achievement

 ◆ Data related to past academic performance

This list presents some of the ways school districts can support schools in their turnaround efforts. You may want to identify additional ways your district can provide support to help you make your turnaround effort a success.

Figure 6.1 is a completed worksheet for identifying district resource needs. Complete this form after you and your school-improvement leadership team have created your school-improvement plan.

Directions: Using the following categories, identify your district resource needs to help with your school-improvement efforts.

General School-Improvement Plan Goals

List your general school-improvement goals below:

- *Provide increased academic support for students.*
- *Increase average daily attendance.*
- *Improve the appearance and cleanliness of the school building and grounds.*

School-Improvement Plan Components	Areas of Possible District Support
• *Support for teachers with improving academic content* • *Seminars for teachers to improve teaching strategies* • *Hiring additional staff to improve building and ground cleanliness* • *Dedicated staff member to follow up with families about student attendance*	• *District office support to understand and unpack standards and develop learning targets and lessons based on the standards* • *Professional development in teaching, learning, and assessment processes* • *Budget resource support to hire additional staff, support with the recruitment and selection process, provide mentoring and support, and meet other new employee needs* • *Budget and personnel support*

Figure 6.1: Sample completed worksheet for identifying possible district resources to assist with a school-turnaround effort.

*Visit **go.SolutionTree.com/schoolimprovement** for a free reproducible version of this figure.*

In figure 6.1, note that the principal has matched components of the school-improvement plan to district resources. It's important to thoroughly consider how the district might support the various elements of the plan to make clear the necessary level of commitment required by the turnaround. Using the worksheet in figure 6.1 can help identify the unanticipated ripple effects or consequences of the school-improvement plan. For example, adding more teachers to reduce class size to give students more individual attention may require the district to manage the recruitment and selection process for these new staff members, provide mentors for them, find office space, provide funding for their salaries and benefits, and so on. The required needs that stem from the decision to hire more teachers are all ripple effects. By taking some time to visualize the whole picture, principals can help the district anticipate and provide resources for additional needs.

Let's see how Anthony DiLeo, the principal of a turnaround elementary school, works with his district to identify helpful resources for his school-turnaround effort.

> Anthony DiLeo, the principal of Brown Elementary School, has been working with his instructional leadership team to identify the most significant areas needing improvement in the school. After several meetings, Principal DiLeo uses this information to develop the following list of initial resource requirements from the school district.
>
> - To improve the working climate at the school, we need assistance moving several negative teachers to other buildings and making the school physically appealing by adding extra custodial staff.
>
> - To improve teachers' instructional capabilities, we need resources for professional development and access to instructional coaches in mathematics and language arts at the school.
>
> - To manage the information flow, we need access to the district's information office for help with print and social media information management.
>
> After developing a document highlighting these needed resources plus the rationale for requests, Principal DiLeo sets up a meeting with the superintendent, assistant superintendent, or other district personnel who can commit district resources to the turnaround school.

While Principal DiLeo will need additional support as the school-improvement plan takes shape, these three resources will help him address some of the initial areas of concern and help him head off distracting issues so he can concentrate on other aspects of his school-improvement plan.

Principal DiLeo decided to ask for this small list of support resources so as not to overwhelm district leadership with a laundry list of needs and to avoid identifying resources that he might eventually find he does not need. However, some principals prefer to compile a more comprehensive plan with most of their needs addressed up front. With either method, it is important to do the following.

- ▸ Clearly identify the needs related to the school-turnaround plan.

- ▸ Provide rationale for the needs. The rationale will help the district to understand the purposes for the resources.

- ▸ Work within the existing district structure and budget when identifying needs. When identifying needed resources, it's important to not request supports that the district cannot provide within its budget.

Many principals find it helpful to develop a plan to communicate the needs and rationale when meeting with the superintendent or school district office personnel to request specific assistance and resources to support the school-turnaround effort.

Meeting With the Superintendent and Other District Office Staff

The following process will assist you as you plan your script to secure the support of the school district in your turnaround effort. Each of the following sections outlines a specific purpose in the conversation. These purposes are (1) set a collaborative tone, (2) provide an overview of the meeting agenda, (3) clarify needs and components of the school-improvement plan, (4) ask for questions and provide clarification, (5) get a commitment or decision, and (6) present a plan for follow-up. As you review the steps in detail, you'll see that we've included some examples of statements that you might make within each step.

Set a Collaborative Tone

It is important to set a collaborative tone when communicating the needs of the school. This shows that you want to work as a team with the district office.

To set a collaborative tone, a school leader might address the superintendent in the following ways.

- ▸ "Thank you for taking the time to meet with me today to discuss this very important topic. I know that together we will be able to develop a plan that will assist the school in this turnaround effort while staying within district budget parameters. I know that your time is valuable, so I outlined some of the major points I'd like to address."

▸ "I appreciate the opportunity for us to be able to meet today. I know you are interested in working together to make our school successful."

Some additional statement starters include:

▸ "Today, as we work together to identify the needed resources for the school-improvement plan at . . ."

▸ "I know that we are on the same page when it comes to the outcome of this school-improvement planning effort . . ."

▸ "I know we are all interested in making sure the school-turnaround plan . . ."

▸ "As you asked, I've taken the data in the school-assessment process and developed the draft of a plan. Today, I'd like to get your feedback and reactions . . ."

▸ "I appreciate the support you've provided so far in the school-turnaround process. Today, I plan to share . . ."

Provide an Overview of the Meeting Agenda

It's important to share the agenda for the meeting with the superintendent and any other district personnel. You may have outlined this in your email message when you asked for the meeting, but take a moment to provide a quick overview of your plan for the meeting.

▸ "During this meeting, I'll share some of the initial needs I've identified for the school, strategies designed to address these needs, and a timeline and cost estimates for the implementation of these strategies. I'll address any questions you have related to this plan, and then together we can prioritize the strategies and ideas we think make the most sense for the school."

▸ "As we go through the school-improvement plan, I'll share the general goals for the school, then the specific strategies we are planning to implement. Once we clarify those strategies, we can discuss any comments, questions, or concerns you may have in relation to our plan."

Some additional statement starters include:

▸ "In our meeting today, I'll share an overview of our school-improvement plan and components of the plan and how they match the needs of the school, and then I'll ask for your thoughts and feedback . . ."

▸ "Earlier, I shared the needs of the school with you. Today, I plan to provide more details related to the actual plan and how . . ."

▸ "Here's what I'm thinking for today. I'll ask you to quickly review the document I've sent in advance, and then I'll ask for areas where you might have questions. Finally . . ."

▸ "For this meeting, let's quickly review the school-improvement needs, and then take a look at the plan I've developed. Once that is complete . . ."

Clarify Needs and Components of the School-Improvement Plan

During this part of the meeting, the principal provides a brief overview of the issues or problems facing the school. This overview allows for everyone to have a common understanding of the issues the school is facing that require turnaround. Example statements include the following.

▸ "Let me take a moment to highlight the major issues Lincoln Middle School is facing. First, our student scores in mathematics . . ."

▸ "Let's start our conversation today by looking at a brief overview of the challenges that have had a negative impact on student learning and achievement at Lincoln Middle School."

Some additional statement starters include:

▸ "Based on the work of our instructional leadership team, here are the major issues that contribute to the lower performance of the school."

▸ "In reviewing all of the data related to the performance of the school, the following five issues seem to stand out the most . . ."

▸ "I've been working with various stakeholder groups to get their perceptions related to issues present at the school. The first part of the plan discussion for today will focus on those issues."

▸ "The major issues that have caused the school to fall behind on its goals to improve student achievement include . . ."

Next, provide a brief review of the outcomes and objectives related to the school's turnaround process to help reinforce that the turnaround plan focuses on broad goals. Providing the outcomes and objectives will also help you later in the meeting when you are justifying some of the activities, techniques, and strategies you'll be asking the district to support. Example statements include the following.

▸ "In order to address the student-learning issues I presented, I have worked together with the instructional leadership team to identify several broad outcomes and objectives for our first year. The first outcome we will be working to accomplish is to . . ."

▸ "The first area we need to address relates to the . . ."

Some additional statement starters include:

▸ "The general goals or outcomes of our plan include . . ."

▸ "Our school-improvement plan is grounded by the following general goals and outcomes . . ."

▸ "In developing our school-improvement plan, we focused on the following three areas."

▸ "As you requested, I worked with our instructional leadership team to identify a set of goals and outcomes to help guide us in the development of our school-improvement plan. These goals and outcomes include . . ."

Now that you have provided an overview of the issues and plans, share the specific strategies you will implement and how they address the outcomes and objectives. Example statements include the following.

▸ "During our first year of implementation, we plan to improve . . . by implementing the following . . ."

▸ "One of the first areas we are trying to change with our school-improvement plan is . . . . We will address that by doing . . ."

Some additional statement starters include:

▸ "Let's take a look at the specific strategies that we plan to use in turning the school around . . ."

▸ "In the document I sent yesterday, I outlined the specific strategies we will implement to begin the turnaround process. Let me start by focusing on those that are designed to . . ."

▸ "In the turnaround plan, there are three themes or major areas where we will begin our work. The first of those areas is . . ."

▸ "Let's go ahead and take a look at the initial strategies we plan to implement . . ."

Be sure to present how your planned strategies match or will address school needs. You may decide to present this information in combination with the strategies and techniques you shared in the previous step. Example statements include the following.

▸ "The professional development we plan to conduct related to _____ will help our teachers to follow up in appropriate ways when _____. In addition, employing a community outreach person will help us . . ."

▸ "As you can see in our plan, we've tried to match each strategy with the larger outcome we are trying to attain in our school-improvement plan."

Some additional statement starters include:

▸ "Strategy one aligns with the first objective of the school-improvement plan since it . . ."

▸ "Since each of the plan techniques fits into one of the objectives, let me share the relationships between these elements . . ."

▸ "As you review the strategies, you'll see that they are color-coded so you can easily see how the needs match the strategies."

▸ "In looking at the first objective, four plan strategies fit directly into it. They are . . ."

Ask for Questions and Provide Clarification

After sharing the information related to the school-improvement plan and needs, be sure to open up the conversation for any questions or needed clarification. Example statements include the following.

▸ "At this point, I'd like to see what questions you may have or what areas may need further clarification."

▸ "After hearing the entire plan, what comments or questions would you like me to address?"

Some additional statement starters include:

▸ "At this point, what questions do you have in relation to the plan strategies and the school-improvement outcomes?"

▸ "On what points can I provide more clarification before we move on to . . . ?"

▸ "In looking at the information I presented in this meeting so far, what questions can I answer?"

▸ "In a minute, I'll ask for your feedback on the school-improvement plan. Before we do that, what areas would you like more clarification on?"

Get a Commitment or Decision

Before ending the meeting, it's important to determine which areas the district will support and which areas they do not yet support. Examples of statements include the following.

▸ "As we close this meeting, what strategies outlined in our plan are you comfortable with and which do you not yet support?"

▸ "After hearing the goals of the plan, what are some of the strategies you support and what others are you concerned about?"

Some additional statement starters include:

▸ "What aspects of the plan can you support? What aspects do you need more clarity or information on before you can support them?"

▸ "You can support steps one through four, but you still have questions about five through seven. What additional information would be helpful as you consider the final steps?"

Present a Plan for Follow-Up

Share your plan to follow up in a few days to see how the decision-making process is progressing. Example statements include the following:

▸ "I know you will need some time to think about this plan and see how it fits into the budget. Let's touch base early next week to discuss it further."

▸ "I've shared a lot of information today. Let's get back together toward the end of the week to discuss it and see what additional questions you may have in relation to the school-improvement plan."

Some additional statement starters include:

▸ "If it's okay with you, we can meet again in two weeks to look at the budget."

▸ "What additional information might be helpful for me to send you as the plan moves forward?"

A map template for planning your own meeting to gain your school district's support for your school-turnaround project appears in figure 6.2. The best kinds of communication maps meet the needs of both the listener and the speaker. If your superintendent or supervisor normally wants to get to the point, with a minimal amount of background information, then you should design your communication map to reflect this preferred style. If your district leaders like a lot of background detail, your communication map

Directions: Use the following template to plan and guide your meeting to gain district support.
Set a collaborative tone:
Provide an overview of the meeting agenda:
Clarify need and components of the school-improvement plan:
Ask for questions and provide clarification:
Get a commitment or decision:
Present a plan for follow-up:
Notes:

Figure 6.2: Template for planning a meeting to obtain district support.

Visit **go.SolutionTree.com/schoolimprovement** for a free reproducible version of this figure.

should reflect that need. If you ensure your communication map addresses the needs of the person or people receiving it, you'll have a greater chance of effectively communicating.

Chapter Summary

At the beginning of this chapter, we looked at the story of Principal Newsome and Superintendent Johnson and their initial planning meeting to determine how the school district would be supporting the school-turnaround process at Noles High School. Let's see how the follow-up meeting went.

> *A few days after their initial meeting, Ms. Newsome and Dr. Johnson met to discuss Principal Newsome's request to have the negative staff members at Noles moved to another school in the district. Dr. Johnson expressed that she thought it would be difficult to move the teachers because of the union contract. She offered to provide additional support for Ms. Newsome in working with these teachers. She also offered to meet individually with these teachers to talk to them about their role at Noles and how they could support the turnaround effort. Ms. Newsome was disappointed but knew that*

Dr. Johnson could not move the teachers. Dr. Johnson and Ms. Newsome agreed to communicate on a weekly basis about these teachers and their impact on the school-turnaround process.

Even though she did not get the teachers moved, Principal Newsome appreciated the fact that the superintendent was keeping a close eye on the situation. If their behaviors negatively impacted the turnaround effort, they could be placed on an improvement plan.

The school district may not be able to meet every need of the school during a turnaround project; if everyone is aware of the school's needs, however, the district will likely address some needs and can work with the principal to develop alternative plans to support turnaround.

In this chapter, we have examined the ways districts can support schools in the turnaround process. Even though the critical role of the district and its active involvement seems clear, if not properly managed, leaders can let important and necessary components of support for successful turnaround slip away. By taking a proactive approach, principals can utilize their school district as an important partner in the school-turnaround process.

In the next chapter, we will examine the elements of the turnaround process. You'll gain an understanding of the concept of school culture, how it can impact the success of your turnaround effort, and how you can enhance it during the turnaround process.

Reflection Questions

As you reflect on the content of this chapter, answer the following questions.

1. What are some of the resources or strategies school districts can provide to support a successful school-turnaround effort? How can these resources enhance the school-improvement plan?

2. Why is it important to identify some of the school district resources that match the school-improvement plan at the beginning of the turnaround process?

3. How can planning the steps in a meeting with school district officials lead to a better collaborative relationship? How will the strategies in this chapter help you to plan an effective meeting?

4. What are some needs you might be able to ask your district to address? How would you plan the conversation so your supervisor understands your needs?

5. If your district cannot address all of the needs you identify, how do you think you'll still be able to move forward with your plan?

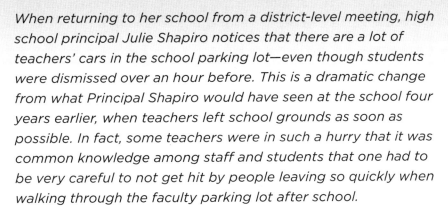

Chapter 7

Maintaining a Positive and Productive Culture

When returning to her school from a district-level meeting, high school principal Julie Shapiro notices that there are a lot of teachers' cars in the school parking lot—even though students were dismissed over an hour before. This is a dramatic change from what Principal Shapiro would have seen at the school four years earlier, when teachers left school grounds as soon as possible. In fact, some teachers were in such a hurry that it was common knowledge among staff and students that one had to be very careful to not get hit by people leaving so quickly when walking through the faculty parking lot after school.

As she enters the office, Principal Shapiro is met by members of her instructional leadership team who remind her that the school is offering extended learning opportunities for students that evening. Members of the instructional leadership team and some of the departmental teams create these opportunities to support students who express concern about upcoming assessments. Many students participate in these assessment support activities, and they tell the teachers they enjoy the opportunities. Teachers also tell Principal Shapiro that they enjoy working with the students in these activities. This is a change from the past, when some teachers said they were reluctant to stay after school to work with students.

Four years before, when Principal Shapiro came to the school, many teachers believed that some students in the school didn't want to learn or couldn't learn. Several teachers even said that it would be a waste of their time to give students extended opportunities. Thankfully, a new, more positive culture emerged, one that makes a difference in student learning. Some negative teachers have long since left the school, but others are still there, and turnaround efforts have helped them change their minds about student potential.

In this brief scenario we see how the culture of Principal Shapiro's school changed from one of negativity and pessimism to one of hope, with a feeling among the staff that teachers can make a difference in the lives of students. Teachers in Principal Shapiro's school have become unwilling to let students fail. The change in their belief system and their way of thinking improved the culture of the school and helped the staff to take action toward their turnaround goals.

In this chapter, we focus on school culture. A school's culture is determined by the beliefs and norms that guide decisions and practices. Without a positive and productive school culture, school turnaround is almost impossible. We will begin by looking at the meaning of school culture in more detail.

Defining School Culture

In *Creative Strategies to Transform School Culture* (Eller & Eller, 2009), we define school culture as "the deep foundation or base that governs many other aspects of the school's operation" (p. 3). School culture is the personality of the school, the frame of reference; it guides thoughts, decisions, and actions. The culture becomes a driving force in how the staff think, helping to guide discussions and actions.

The culture of a school is stable and consistent over time. Changing school culture can be somewhat difficult, like changing the course of a large ship moving in a certain direction. Unlike climate, culture has a certain amount of inertia that keeps it stable. If it's negative or toxic, it will continue to be toxic unless acted on with sustained efforts and strategies. Three types of school culture can be present in schools: (1) positive or productive culture, (2) toxic culture, and (3) status quo culture.

Three Types of School Culture

While each school culture is unique and based on the specific conditions at the school, unique features often exist under the umbrella of one of the three core types. Let's look more closely at these types.

Positive or Productive School Culture

A positive or productive culture is desirable. It is a culture where a sense of trust and community exists. Teachers engage in collaborative work. Most problems are viewed as opportunities. Teachers see one another as resources and work interdependently. The principal nurtures teacher leadership by appropriately developing the staff, providing opportunities for growth, working collaboratively with teachers, developing a shared vision, and following up with staff to ensure everyone is contributing to the shared vision. In this type of culture, leaders address problems proactively. Staff members support one another. A positive or productive culture needs constant support and maintenance to keep it vibrant and moving forward. In such a culture, a feeling that everyone is in it together prevails.

Many attributes contribute to make a school's culture positive and productive. A culture does not need to have every attribute in place, but it does require a critical mass of elements in order to be seen and experienced as positive and productive.

Toxic School Culture

A toxic culture is one where staff members either openly work against one another or, because of extreme chaos, cannot focus beyond their own survival. In toxic cultures, enough negativity exists that it gets in the way of success with students. Formal and informal leadership in the school squashes new ideas, works against collaboration, and does not support interdependent relationships. Negativity permeates the school. Schools with toxic cultures are unpleasant places to work and cause a high level of staff despair, hopelessness, and turnover. Staff members who cannot leave continue to fuel the negativity.

In a toxic culture, there is no unified vision. Everyone is left to determine their own focus. The principal is autocratic or micromanaging. He or she does not develop the leadership skills of the faculty. Faculty members cannot make decisions without permission. Staff complain about students, families, and other staff members. They don't generate possible solutions to problems. This lack of a sense of control permeates student learning. Faculty members openly disagree on ideas, strategies, and other issues, and the disagreement takes a personal tone. There are no strategies in place for conflict resolution. Teachers in toxic cultures believe that some students can't learn and that teachers can't effectively navigate outside factors influencing student success.

A culture can be toxic even if it does not exhibit all of these factors; the degree to which several factors are present can determine the level of toxicity. For example, a small but strong and negative group of faculty members can override a larger, more positive group and make the culture toxic. The level of toxicity can be on a continuum. Identifying the strength and prevalence of the negative attributes should help the principal and the instructional leadership team determine where to target the interventions to begin to change the culture.

Status Quo School Culture

A third type of culture prevalent in schools is a status quo culture. In a status quo culture, leaders or a critical mass of staff members believe that things are working well. They believe most students are achieving goals, there are few classroom-management concerns, most parents and students seem happy with the school, and staff members are able to utilize the strategies and techniques they have employed for years. The school relies on its reputation and what has worked in the past to deal with problems even though these strategies may not be solving current problems. Everyone seems happy, but they are unaware of the fact that the school has gradually fallen behind or is becoming out of touch with its reality.

Status quo cultures can be dangerous and difficult to change. Without a sense of urgency or the rationale for change, staff in a status quo culture will resist change efforts. Because people in the school think they are doing well, they see no reason for change. The leader or instructional leadership team will need to help a critical mass of the staff see the need for the change in order to help them move forward.

Status quo cultures are also dangerous because they can move toward toxic status if a change in outside conditions makes it more difficult for them to maintain some level of success using only their existing skills. Because they have talked themselves into thinking they are good, they believe that negative changes are the fault of students or families. Leaders and staff don't take ownership of issues.

A Continuum of School Culture

School culture can be placed on a continuum based on its level of effectiveness or on the influence of its negativity using the data-gathering process described in this book. Viewing your school on a continuum (see figure 7.1) is helpful since very few schools fit perfectly into one of the three types of culture. For example, a positive and productive school might have a small group of toxic staff members. The school culture would not be 100 percent positive or productive and would fit on the continuum slightly to the left of the positive or productive designation. Conversely, a school may think its culture is totally toxic but further analysis might reveal that there are some positive elements in place. That school could be rated slightly to the right of the toxic side, motivating staff to move further right. Viewing a school on a continuum allows leaders and staff members to work toward change.

Assessing the Culture of a School

To assess the culture of your school, you and your instructional leadership team must look beyond feelings or impressions to gather tangible data to help you define the present state of the culture. It is also important to use some sort of a model to define the important attributes to measure.

Figure 7.1: Continuum of school culture types.

Visit **go.SolutionTree.com/schoolimprovement** *for a free reproducible version of this figure.*

One model of organizational culture we have found helpful is in the work of Edgar Schein. Schein's groundbreaking methods help articulate the attributes that contribute to organizational culture. In his book *Organizational Culture and Leadership*, Schein (2016) notes that the culture of a group:

> Can be defined as a pattern of shared basic assumptions that the group learned as it solved its problems of external adaptation and internal integration, that has worked well enough to be considered valid and therefore, to be taught to new members as the correct way to perceive, think, and feel in relation to those problems. (p. 6)

Schein (2016) makes several key points.

▸ Culture is a pattern of assumptions and behaviors in use or consideration in the organization.

▸ The assumptions (behaviors and strategies) have worked for the organization in the past.

▸ The assumptions (behaviors and strategies) are passed on to new members who join the organization.

These points are helpful in thinking about assessing the culture of a school. The assessment should be based on both observable actions and on patterns of thought. Schein's (2016) work focuses on three major attributes of organizational culture that fit these key points and make the culture assessable. He calls these attributes "three levels of analysis related to culture" (p. 17): (1) artifacts, (2) espoused beliefs, and (3) basic underlying assumptions. We elaborate on these levels in the following list.

1. **Artifacts** should be visible and observable products in the school. Artifacts might include posted items (such as student work and materials in the teachers' lounge), cleanliness and organization of the school's physical spaces, whether or not the school entrance is welcoming, and other observable elements.

2. **Espoused beliefs** are the thoughts or beliefs people say they follow. Espoused beliefs might include the content of the mission and vision statements, the content of the written school rules, what people say the mission of the school is, and other spoken or publicly shared ideas and information.

3. **Basic underlying assumptions** are the thoughts or frames of reference that really govern a culture. These basic underlying assumptions might include the actual behaviors of leaders and staff members, the unspoken rules and procedures, what people in the culture really think, and other informal thoughts.

In our work with schools, we use the iceberg visual in figure 7.2 to help educators understand the relationship between the three attributes of culture.

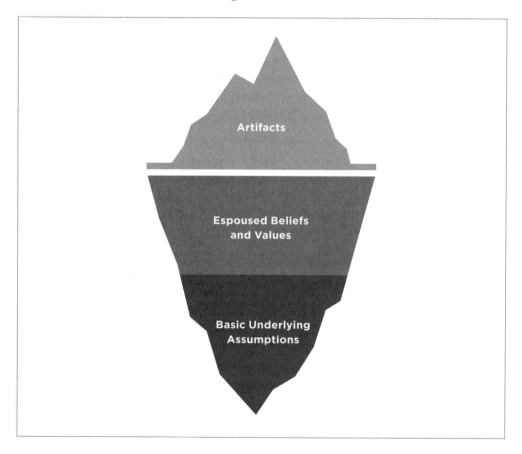

Figure 7.2: Visual representation of school culture attributes.

Like the tip of the iceberg, artifacts are the most visible. Espoused beliefs lie just below the surface and are not visible, but they make up a large portion of the culture (like the middle of the iceberg). Underlying assumptions are at the base of the culture and, like with an iceberg, the base controls the direction and what's visible and comprises the critical mass of the culture.

It may be helpful to conduct an audit on your school culture. We can provide an example of a school culture audit in figure 7.3. In figure 7.3, we see how most of the indicators of culture are in the positive and productive column. There are a few areas in the status quo column, but the school staff are working to address those areas.

Directions: Respond to the following questions to assess your school's culture.

1. What artifacts do you see around the school in offices, halls, classrooms, on the website, and so on, that define the organization?

   Student work is posted in classrooms. Teachers have posted the banner from the university each attended above the door. There are welcome signs around the school. Teachers are in the halls talking with students during passing times. Most of the artifacts are only in English, however.

2. What kinds of behaviors do you observe in meetings, formal events, in day-to-day operations, and so on, that seem to define the organization?

   Meetings begin with an ice-breaker activity. People vary their seating in meetings so they talk to staff members beyond just their closest colleagues. An agenda guides each meeting. Some teachers are allowed to come late to meetings, though.

3. What are the espoused beliefs and values that the organization communicates or follows?

   The posted motto of the school is "every child, every day." Teachers shared how they put students first. There is a no-suspension-from-class policy in place.

4. How does the organization rationalize statements, actions, and so on, that are not congruent with the espoused beliefs and values?

   The instructional leadership team members shared how they are working with teachers who did not follow the "every child, every day" motto. Professional development mini-sessions are offered to help teachers learn classroom-management skills to avoid asking disruptive students to leave class and go to the office.

5. What are some of the unwritten rules and procedures that staff need to follow in order to be successful in this organization?

   Teachers reported during interviews that the principal follows up with teachers who don't follow the "every child, every day" motto.

Figure 7.3: Completed worksheet to assess the culture of your school.

continued →

Use the following chart to collect the data about the culture of your school.			
	Type of Culture		
	Positive and Productive	Toxic	Status Quo
Artifacts	Welcome signs, university banners		Signs and posters are only in English.
Espoused Beliefs	"Every child, every day" motto at the school		Not all teachers follow the motto every day; team members are working with them to understand and adopt the motto.
Basic Underlying Assumptions	Principal supports the school change process by confronting staff who operate counter to the culture.		
Notes: Most teachers express optimism about working at the school.			
Plan for improving or maintaining culture:			
Continue to work on getting everyone on board with living the school motto. Work to help all students (including students who recently have come to the school from other countries) feel welcome by including posters and messages reflecting their languages and cultures.			

Visit **go.SolutionTree.com/schoolimprovement** *for a free reproducible version of this figure.*

Instructional leadership team members can conduct an assessment similar to the one in the example by doing the following.

- Conducting a walk-around assessment, making note of the artifacts they notice in the school

- Holding discussions, focus groups, or interviews with collaborative teams to get feedback and perspectives about underlying assumptions and espoused values in the school

- Holding discussions or focus groups or administering surveys with groups of students to find out their perceptions of the culture

- Administering surveys or holding focus group discussions with parents to have them share their perceptions of the culture of the school

Once data have been gathered, the principal and instructional leadership team can meet to discuss what they've learned as a result of the assessment. Using an open discussion format allows everyone to understand the data and begin to draw conclusions related to school culture.

An important idea to keep in mind is the presence or absence of congruence (alignment) in the data. For example, if teachers report a strong collaborative working culture at the school and the team finds evidence or examples of how teachers have worked together to solve problems, the team's perceptions are probably accurate. On the other hand, if teachers report strong collaborative relationships, but evidence shows that teachers rarely work together, then further investigation is required.

Let's see how Mary Martin, a middle school principal, works with her staff to perform a school culture audit.

Middle school principal Mary Martin asks her instructional leadership team to complete a school culture audit. The team spends a week gathering data and then meets to discuss the results. This team collects school culture data by interviewing other teachers, conducting focus group conversations, and by doing a school walk-around to look for evidence of artifacts and other activities.

Several team members note that the school's mission statement mentions the value of diversity and working collaboratively to ensure success for all students, but the team also notes that the directional and school expectation signs posted throughout the school are written in English only, even though a significant percentage of the student population is Spanish speaking. Team members also mention that some of the teachers they spoke with informally said they did not support instruction in languages other than English.

After analyzing the data sources, the school instructional leadership team concludes that the mission statement and the other data sources are not congruent with the actual practices and beliefs at the school. The espoused values (the mission) do not match the artifacts or the underlying assumptions (real beliefs, values, and actions) of the faculty.

As a result of this informal culture assessment, the team decides to focus its initial school culture improvement efforts on helping teachers better understand the way the English learner program works and to add more bilingual signage to the school. They also decide to hold an open forum at the next faculty meeting to share the results of the school culture assessment and have an open discussion about the findings.

In this example, we see how the instructional leadership team analyzed and used the data to make decisions about the present condition of the culture and to define where they plan to start to refine the culture. The staff at this school are accustomed to having open conversations about issues, so that is one reason why the team decided to employ that strategy. If the staff could not handle potentially controversial open conversations, they may have met with small groups or departments or sent the information out to faculty in written form.

Once a leader or instructional leadership team has conducted an assessment of the school's culture, it is time to take specific steps to move the school further to the right on the continuum, or implement strategies to support a school that already embodies a positive and productive culture.

Leading a Positive and Productive School Culture

Leaders who are successful at building positive and productive school cultures embody certain characteristics. These include focusing on the good, showing positive personal regard, actively listening, giving feedback, making the work play, celebrating and sharing good news, seeking to understand others, and setting clear expectations. We elaborate on these elements in the following sections.

Focus on the Good

Since schools are made up of a variety of people from different backgrounds, with different interests, values, and so on, it's not surprising that everyone doesn't get along all the time. As a leader, sometimes you may have to remind yourself to find the good in everyone. This shift in outlook goes far in building a positive school climate.

A leader might think of a staff member who questions everything as a pain or as someone who obstructs progress; however, if you are able to change your outlook to see the staff member's skepticism as a gift that helps the rest of the staff see potential problems in a plan, you may develop a different opinion of that person. Being able to step back and analyze people and situations can help you see all sides of an issue.

We must clarify—we're not asking you to like everyone or overlook all challenging or irritating behaviors in others. Rather, thinking about each staff member's value and contribution to the school may help you more easily make them feel valued and welcomed, supporting a positive school climate. This focus on the good is important in school turnaround. Building on strengths, rather than focusing on negatives, is a great way to refocus the school.

Show Positive Personal Regard

How we interact with and communicate with one another builds good will that is needed during the school-turnaround process. When greeting staff members, ask how they are doing, and convey a sense of caring about them—such as we emphasize in chapter 4 in the discussion of the care factor.

We once visited a school where the staff make it a practice to greet one another in the hallways and common spaces. Even if they see one another multiple times during a day, they say hello. This simple act helps build a productive climate and nurtures staff members when they encounter difficulties in their school-turnaround projects. They are able to access one another's strengths to get through the difficult issues.

In another school, teachers were so occupied by their daily tasks that they did not take the time to use cordial greetings. Two teachers could meet in the hallway and not even acknowledge each other. The lack of personal regard contributed to a negative work climate. When the staff at this school faced an issue, people retreated and decided to take care of themselves. Because the leader had not focused on building the foundations of a positive climate, staff members could not count on one another for support.

Actively Listen

Active listening is a set of skills a listener uses to understand the speaker's message. Maintaining eye contact, temporarily suspending judgment, acknowledging the speaker's thoughts and feelings, and other strategies all contribute to listeners' communicating their interest in and the importance of the speaker's message.

Leaders can use active listening strategies to show staff that they care about their opinions. It also gives turnaround leaders the opportunity to get many ideas on the table before selecting the ones that have the greatest potential for success. Active listening can result in information and perspectives that help the listener solve his or her own problems as well.

Two keys to active listening are focusing on the other person and avoiding inserting your own ideas and opinions into the conversation until the speaker has completed expressing his or her thoughts. By providing appropriate eye contact, you convey that the speaker is important. When appropriate eye contact is coupled with receptive body language (facing the other person, leaning in when they speak, and so on), it sends a powerful message and supports a positive work climate. It's also important to occasionally acknowledge what the other person is saying. By nodding your head, saying

"Yes," and paraphrasing and reflecting, you make the speaker feel valued as the conversation unfolds.

When listening actively, ask open-ended questions to help the speaker think more deeply about the issue and clarify main points. Some open-ended questions could include, "Why do you think this happened?" or "What did you notice when you approached the student about the issue?" By using open-ended questioning, active listeners help to establish and reinforce a working climate that accepts and values people's opinions. Active listening helps to minimize the defensive tone that is often present in negative school cultures.

During school turnaround, active listening can help leaders maintain a sense of calm when potentially stressful events occur, as well as generate ideas for problem solving. Active listening is an important skill for leaders as well as for the school instructional leadership team, departmental and grade-level teams, collaborative groups, the staff, and other stakeholders in the school.

Give Feedback

Accepting the views of another without judgement is important, but so is giving feedback. Feedback helps people understand how they are doing and whether they are meeting workplace expectations. For feedback to be effective, it has to have the following characteristics.

- **Accuracy:** Feedback should be based on correct information.
- **Specificity:** Clear and specific feedback is the easiest to understand and follow.
- **Timeliness:** Feedback provided relatively soon after the event is the most valuable.
- **A focus on behavior:** This focus must be on the observable or describable behavior you noticed or saw.
- **A plan of action:** Reinforcing feedback conveys that the individual should continue to implement the behavior or strategy, and developmental feedback conveys the recommended change in strategies or technique.

Most feedback either reinforces or strengthens productive behavior or redirects or changes unproductive behavior. In either case, feedback reinforces a positive climate because staff understand expectations and how to reach them.

Make the Work Play

Successful turnaround leaders find ways to make work fun. Holding contests, giving out funny awards, participating in teambuilding exercises, and implementing fun projects, such as making videos to welcome students, explain procedures, highlight staff success, and promote school culture, are all ways to help people have fun in the workplace. These strategies also help staff to recharge and prepare for the additional hard work they'll need to do for school turnaround.

Celebrate and Share Good News

Celebrations serve a crucial function in school turnaround. As we discussed earlier in the book, during the turnaround process, staff are buoyed by quick wins. Celebrating quick wins and long-term successes rewards a job well done, and helps propel further changes. During school turnaround, successes need to be celebrated soon and often.

One technique for sharing good news involves asking several staff members to come to a faculty meeting prepared to share good news that is either personal or professional. At first, people may be reluctant to share, but as the strategy becomes a recurring element of subsequent meetings, people will become more comfortable and may decide to share more personal information. The strategy builds a positive school culture by helping people learn important information about one another (Eller, 2004).

Good news can also be spread using the school's social media accounts, or posted on a section of the school website dedicated to promoting good news. For example, we know of several schools that have produced informational videos set to popular music. These videos are motivating to watch and because they are set to popular music and contain school personnel and students, teachers and students enjoy watching them. We know of a school that has its collaborative teams make videos showing their team norms and positive aspects of their working relationships.

Turnaround schools can also feature good news announcements at schoolwide events and assemblies. These positive celebrations help build the emotional enthusiasm gained from the positive progress the school is making toward reaching its school-turnaround goals.

Seek to Understand Others

Leaders and staff members can benefit from learning more about their own processes for thinking and understanding information, and about the processes of others. Commercially available assessments help individuals to identify their attributes so that the group can learn more about one another, appreciating one another's strengths and limitations in order to work together more productively. Some of these might include the Myers-Briggs personality assessment, the DiSC profile assessment, the Personality Compass, and others. When issues arise with turnaround and people start to become frustrated, they are able to think critically about how they think and process information and hopefully shift their mindset from negativity or close-mindedness to positivity or open-mindedness. Staff can also identify strategies to use in working through conflicts that arise while further appreciating diversity in other ways of thinking.

Set Clear Expectations

To develop a positive climate and ultimately a productive culture, people need to be clear about their expectations for one another. This is especially important in school-turnaround efforts when many significant changes are happening at once.

The following activity, called What Do We Expect? (Eller & Eller, 2009), provides a way for people to get their expectations out in the open. This strategy, outlined in seven steps, helps build a positive and productive school climate and culture. It is useful for when a new principal arrives, or at the start of a new initiative—any time when clarification of expectations is necessary.

1. Gather all staff together to talk about the importance of clear expectations.

2. Divide staff members into small groups of five or six people and ask each group to respond to the following questions on chart paper:

   - What do we expect from our leader?
   - What do we expect from our faculty, staff, or team members?
   - What do we expect from ourselves as individuals?

3. Once all groups have completed their lists, they should report their work to the larger group.

4. When all groups have shared, ask group members to summarize what they heard each individual group report and what the group lists have in common.

5. Once all of the groups have reported, share your expectations of the staff. Ask the small teams to meet again and talk about the expectations. Each team should identify any expectations they

may have trouble supporting if enacted at the school. For such expectations, there should be more discussion to understand the issue and try to get the staff members to support it.

6. Each team then reports on the leader expectation discussion. The leader listens to the expectations and does not comment whether or not he or she agrees until all of the expectations have been shared. The final items are listed based on the collaborative discussion between the leader and the faculty.

7. All the lists are typed reflecting the combined expectations and distributed at a future faculty meeting for faculty reaction and final adoption. The adoption process involves staff reading the lists, making sure any questions or expectations needing clarification are addressed. Once everything is clarified, the staff adopt the expectations. The adoption process can be conducted by a vote, through consensus processes, or using whatever decision-making process the staff normally use.

Chapter Summary

In the beginning of the chapter, we see how Principal Julie Shapiro improved the culture of her school. Let's take a look at how the culture at her school gets even better.

The teachers in Principal Julie Shapiro's high school work hard to help students learn and grow. Many volunteer to stay after school and provide extended learning opportunities for students. They take a lot of pride in the fact that they are working together as collaborative teams to identify and implement high-impact instructional strategies. Collaborative teams set learning goals for the team members and share ideas related to high-impact instructional strategies. Teachers on these collaborative teams volunteer to take videos of themselves implementing high-impact strategies, and then they share the videos during their collaborative team meetings. As each teacher shares his or her video, the remainder of the collaborative team provides feedback and coaching for the teacher sharing the video.

As teams and individuals continue to support one another, everybody sets even higher professional goals, stretching one another as professionals. Teachers who are not interested in growing professionally discover they are out of sync with their colleagues. Some of these teachers decide to step up their professional goals while others may leave to work elsewhere. The culture of the school is transformed from one where teachers are just doing their jobs to one where teachers do everything possible to help their students grow. This change in culture is very evident to the students and to new teachers who decide to join the team. Julie has planted a seed that is starting to grow into a mighty oak!

As Principal Shapiro's story shows, making the right investments in developing a sound, strong, positive culture is important for a turnaround school. Julie started the process when she came to the school, but the teachers took it from there, helping one another grow and learn. Soon, the positive culture was contagious and supported itself.

In this chapter, we examined the concept of school culture and how school climate affects school culture, how leaders can assess school culture at their own schools, and how to improve culture for successful turnaround.

In chapter 8, "Building Capacity," you'll learn important and practical strategies to understand to build staff capacity, maximizing your success as a turnaround leader.

Reflection Questions

As you reflect on the content of this chapter, answer the following questions.

1. What are the definitions of school culture and school climate? What do the two concepts have in common, and how are they different?

2. What are the three major types of school culture? What are the attributes of each, and how do they work to promote or get in the way of school change?

3. What are some artifacts that can help leaders understand their school cultures? How can espoused values and underlying assumptions help leaders understand the culture?

4. How will you move forward with evaluating the culture in your school? How will school culture change as you work with your school staff to flip your school?

Chapter 8

Building Capacity

Val Hawkins, a new teacher at Everly Elementary School, is working with a group of students who face many challenges as learners. She works hard each day to make her lessons interesting and relevant for her students. Without the resources her principal, Norm Schultz, provides, she would feel overwhelmed.

At the beginning of the school year, Principal Schultz met with Ms. Hawkins to identify the strengths he saw in her teaching and to get her perspective on her strengths. Together they worked on a plan to help her set several professional growth goals for the year, make a connection with a more veteran teacher, and attend some professional development sessions. Principal Shultz plans to stop by Ms. Hawkins's classroom at least once a week to observe and provide feedback on her teaching progress. He wants Ms. Hawkins to concentrate on a core set of strategies designed to help her students stay engaged in the instruction and to focus on implementing the common assessments that her colleagues developed during the previous school year.

Although the work is not easy, Ms. Hawkins feels that she is going to get the assistance she needs to do a good job at Everly Elementary.

In this example, we see how Principal Schultz gives Ms. Hawkins specific attention to help her set and work to attain professional growth goals. However, development work is not just for new teachers. Turnaround principals should work with every teacher in the building to help him or her grow professionally and learn the essential skills and strategies he or she needs in order to support and motivate students. If teachers are not improving their instructional skills so that they have more to offer students, the turnaround will not work.

In this chapter, you'll learn how to use interactive supervision to coach teachers to higher levels of performance and effectiveness. You'll learn strategies for selecting focused teaching and learning strategies, methods for using regular observations and feedback, how to track progress, the types of professional development turnaround leaders might implement, and how to find time for professional learning.

We begin with a discussion of the school leader's role in identifying and reinforcing necessary skill development and using that information to supervise—rather than simply evaluate—growth.

Leading Learning

In order to help teachers improve their instruction, school leaders must lead staff learning, shaping behavior and the acquisition of skills toward the goal of increased student achievement. Let's look at a scenario in which a school principal does not help a teacher improve behaviors and develop better skills, because, in this case, the principal does not move beyond simply reinforcing existing behavior.

> John Casey, a middle school principal, gets ready to implement the district's teacher-evaluation process during the upcoming school year. He sends out an email to the entire teaching staff letting everyone know they will be evaluated. He is required to formally observe each continuing contract teacher at least once during the school year and each probationary teacher at least three times. Observations and feedback must be based on the school district's teaching checklist. At the end of the year, Principal Casey completes a scoring form, rating each teacher and his or her performance.

> Principal Casey starts the year by setting up the observation schedule. The teachers know the dates and times of their observations at least a month in advance. As he conducts observations, he notices that teachers have prepared each lesson well. The students are on track and well-behaved. Students seem successful in relation to the learning targets of each lesson.

> At the end of the year, Principal Casey's ratings of each teacher are similar. Most teachers receive marks of proficient on the required criteria. He provides very little direction for needed changes or refinements. Veteran teachers have been getting these kinds of scores for years. Instruction remains pretty much the same from year to year.

In this scenario, we see the classic teacher-evaluation process play out. Principal Casey follows the requirements set out in the district teacher-evaluation guidebook. He performs the basic tasks necessary to comply with the requirements. As a result of his actions, the teachers in his school maintain the status quo; nobody grows or learns.

Let's see how Melanie Hawthorne, an elementary principal, approaches teacher evaluation differently.

Melanie Hawthorne, the principal of Bucknell Elementary School, believes teacher supervision is one of her most important responsibilities. She understands that helping teachers build sound instructional skills will help eliminate some student discipline issues, resolve parental concerns, and improve the school's culture of success.

Principal Hawthorne works with her instructional leadership team to identify six priority areas within the school district's core teaching performance expectations. Her teachers are required to work on all areas, but the six she identifies are the most essential. The instructional leadership team works with grade-level collaborative teams to support them in learning new strategies to implement the six priority areas.

In the early fall, Principal Hawthorne meets with all teachers to discuss the district's core expectations and the six priority areas so that everyone understands them. She lets the staff know that she will be doing informal walkthroughs to provide feedback on the six priority areas. She helps those teachers who are not on the formal evaluation cycle develop professional growth goals based on the six priority areas. She meets with teachers on the formal evaluation cycle to discuss how the six priority areas will be a part of this process.

As the year progresses, Principal Hawthorne does informal walkthroughs each week, visiting each classroom, on average, at least once every two weeks. After each visit, she meets briefly with the teacher to gain his or her perspective and provide feedback. She keeps track of the results of each visit and knows how everyone is doing in relation to the six priority areas. She takes this into consideration as she plans her faculty meetings and professional growth sessions. She uses these events to provide additional opportunities for her teachers to grow in their instructional skills.

In the second example, we see a very different level of interest and commitment to teacher learning and growth. Principal Hawthorne uses walkthrough observations and feedback as tools to help teachers grow their skills. The instructional leadership team supports collaborative teams. Principal

Hawthorne uses her leadership skills to truly impact teacher growth, rather than just evaluate their performance.

Supervising Versus Evaluating

In education, leaders often spend a lot of time measuring without doing anything with the data they gather from the measurements. Evaluation is just one part of supervision. Effective evaluation means that we not only evaluate a teacher (rate his or her ability at using a certain skill or strategy), but also use what we discover during evaluation to focus their work with teachers—to supervise their growth and development.

In *Score to Soar* (Eller & Eller, 2015), we discuss how the role of evaluator or measurer fits into the greater scope of supervision.

Teacher supervision includes the following.

▸ Evaluating, rating, or grading performance

▸ Gathering information to assist in the development of individuals

▸ Gathering information to assist in the development of a group of employees or the entire school

Even though evaluating and measuring are an important part of effectively supervising employees, they are not the only strategies principals should use. The last two points in the list, gathering information to assist in the development of individuals and gathering information to assist in the development of a group, are crucial to the success of a turnaround process. If teachers are to ensure success for all students, leaders need to help both individuals and the entire teaching staff learn and implement new teaching strategies.

Selecting Focused Teaching and Learning Strategies

Successful turnaround principals work to identify the most promising, research-based teaching strategies. While there are many sources for effective teaching strategies, those leaders choose to focus on should be the ones deemed most essential based on specific needs of students. Resources such as *Visible Learning* by John Hattie (2008) aid leaders in this task. Hattie identifies effective teaching strategies through a meta-analysis, or by rating or ranking common teaching behaviors from high (larger effect sizes) to low (lower effect sizes). This ranking allows teachers and leaders to quickly locate the teaching strategies that have the highest probability of raising student achievement (Hattie, 2008).

The key is to prioritize the use of teaching strategies based on their impact and student needs. For example, one of the teaching strategies that Hattie (2011) finds has a high impact (or effect size) is classroom discussion. The rationale for this teaching strategy is that by actively participating in a discussion, students hear others describe the material, have a chance to present their thoughts on the material, are able to present counterpoints, and so on. It would seem to make sense that a school should adopt this teaching strategy and require that all teachers use discussions in their classrooms. However, focusing right away on increasing classroom discussion may not make sense in some settings.

In a particular school, some students lack the basic behavior skills needed to hold a productive discussion or have not had a chance to gain the confidence to feel comfortable in sharing their ideas with a larger group. What if many of the students in a school have recently immigrated and lack the skills to communicate together as a large group? In these situations, it may be better for the school instructional leadership team and the principal to have the teachers focus on some other foundational skills that could *lead to* effective discussion skills. Students would need to know how to clearly share their ideas, listen to each other's ideas, keep the discussion on topic, and draw conclusions from the ideas expressed in the discussion. The school would be helping students by building foundational skills first, then implementing discussion skills when appropriate.

Figure 8.1 (page 154) is a completed template to assist you and your instructional leadership team in identifying essential teaching skills for your school.

The process in figure 8.1 helps the principal and the instructional leadership team to visualize and think through the process of identifying teaching strategies and matching them to student learning needs. Thinking through processes visually helps a group to slow down and process the steps carefully.

In the example in figure 8.1, you can see how the principal and the instructional leadership team thought through the possible teaching strategies before focusing on a few to implement as an entire school. Also, the school in the sample is taking small steps in implementing the new teaching strategies. You may decide that because of the characteristics, personalities, or present skill level of your teachers that you and your school can start using more complex teaching strategies sooner than in this example. Once leaders have identified essential teaching strategies, they can move on to designing processes and supports to help teachers master them.

Directions: Use the following template to help you identify the essential teaching strategies you think should be the focus of your work with teachers.

List the school-improvement goals and strategies that directly relate to improving student learning.

- *Students will increase their ability to use reason in developing an argument.*
- *Students will increase their ability to write logically and sequentially.*
- *Students will be able to increase their achievement in mathematics processing skills.*

For each goal listed, write the student skills and the teaching strategies that would enable the students to meet the goals.

Student Learning Goal	Student Skills Needed to Attain Goal	Teaching Strategies Needed to Help Students Reach Goal
• *Reasoning* • *Writing logically and sequentially* • *Using mathematics processing skills*	• *Develop complete thoughts, use information from others, and suspend judgement.* • *Connect thoughts, evaluate information, and order information.* • *Use set processes for problem solving and reflect on process and make refinements.*	• *Using classroom discussion, metacognition* • *Helping students reflect on work in small peer teams* • *Directly teaching processes, providing students with process task cards, and using small-group reflection after completion of mathematics problems*

List the subskills or prerequisite skills students need to learn in order for the identified teaching strategies to be successful.

Teaching Strategy	Student Prerequisite Skills
• *Classroom discussion* • *Working on small teams* • *Direct teaching*	• *Staying on task, controlling voice levels, returning to task, and using a metacognition process for thinking* • *Staying on task, controlling voice levels, returning to task in the larger group* • *Taking good notes, focusing during teaching*

Stage I: Select two or three teaching strategies to implement over the next three to four months. Prioritize those strategies that either address student prerequisite skills or that teachers can easily implement.

- *Helping students learn appropriate voice levels for working in small groups*
- *Helping teachers implement short-term group discussions*
- *Helping teachers provide clear instruction and present notes in content areas*

Stage II: Select two to three teaching strategies to implement on a longer-term basis (four months to a year). Prioritize those strategies that build on the strategies implemented in stage I.

- *Helping teachers implement long-term group work*
- *Helping teachers design and present clear process lessons (teaching students how to do complex processes)*

Figure 8.1: Template and sample responses for identifying essential or important teaching skills.

*Visit **go.SolutionTree.com/schoolimprovement** for a free reproducible version of this figure.*

Using Regular Observations and Feedback

In the second scenario at the beginning of the chapter, elementary principal Melanie Hawthorne provides regular and focused feedback for her teachers after short, informal, walkthrough observations that she does frequently. These regular visits and feedback let the teachers know how they are doing in relation to the expectations. The regular visits and feedback are designed to help them grow in a supervisory manner. The longer, less-frequent formal observations are designed to measure or evaluate her teachers.

Some principals, like Principal Hawthorne, use a walkthrough process in which they plan to visit each classroom on a weekly basis for three to five minutes, focusing on specific signs of strategy implementation, while other leaders choose to set up a more concrete schedule. No matter what the specifics of the process, the goal is to get snapshots of the classroom on which to base feedback. Such observation allows the principal to do the following.

- ▸ Obtain more concise and regular views of the classroom during different times to enable a view of the beginning, middle, and end of a lesson.

- ▸ Focus on a small number of teaching strategies rather than the larger list of district teacher-performance criteria.

- ▸ Spend more time holding conversations about teaching and learning, and coaching teachers on their professional practices.

- ▸ Get a feel for what is happening in the school.

- ▸ Help teachers to see the big picture, and see students in multiple settings.

- ▸ Reduce the anxiety associated with classroom visits.

- ▸ Gain more accurate information about teaching, rather than observing only prepared lessons once or twice a year.

As a busy school leader, the thought of spending even more time in classrooms probably seems daunting. Developing strategies for planning regular classroom visits will help you manage your time effectively and make classroom visits a priority, as will providing specific types of feedback.

Strategies for Planning Regular Classroom Visits

Regular classroom visits send a message that you care about teaching and learning, and that you support teachers in their growth. Making classroom visits and the corresponding follow-up conversations a priority will help in managing the time needed for this task. If you don't make classroom visits a priority, other things will take up your time and it will be hard to get into classrooms and help guide instructional improvement.

But how is this possible with all of the other important things a principal has to attend to in a given day? Following are some strategies you may find helpful in managing time to get into classrooms on a regular basis.

▸ When you do your weekly planning, block out time for classroom walkthrough visits first so they become a priority. If you plan everything else first, the visits will get pushed off.

▸ Publicly announce that visiting classrooms is a priority for you, and remind teachers and staff often. This helps them understand why you might not be available in the office or why they might see you out in the halls on a regular basis.

▸ Work with your administrative assistant to keep observational time sacred so you are not interrupted or called back to the office (unless it's an emergency). Your administrative assistant should share with callers or people stopping by the office to see you that you are observing in classrooms. This message reinforces the importance of instructional improvement throughout the school community.

▸ Keep moving as you work through your classroom observation schedule. If you've allowed ten minutes for each classroom, move on when that time is up. It's easy to lose track of time in the classroom as lessons get interesting, so you may want to allow yourself a little flex time so you don't get off schedule. Some principals set a schedule and adhere to it no matter what happens. You have to decide what form of scheduling works best for you. The important thing is that you are in classrooms and supporting teachers on a regular basis.

▸ Since you will be visiting a lot of classrooms and observing a lot of lessons, you will need an efficient way to keep track of the information you are compiling so you can provide feedback to your teachers. Some principals prefer to take their laptops or tablets with them, while others use their cell phones. Some principals prefer to keep their notes in a hard copy format. Whatever form you use, it's a good idea to keep track of the following information related to the observations.

  ◆ Date and time of each observation

  ◆ Focus of the lesson (content focus)

  ◆ Some points or main steps you observed happening in the lesson

  ◆ Positive or productive teaching strategies you saw

  ◆ Areas for growth or possible refinement to share with the teacher

An outline of how record keeping might look (in spreadsheet form) appears in figure 8.2.

Teacher Name	Date and Time of Observation	Lesson Focus	Lesson Steps or Points	Positive or Productive Teaching Strategies	Areas for Growth or Refinement

Figure 8.2: Sample format for record keeping related to regular lesson observations.

*Visit **go.SolutionTree.com/schoolimprovement** for a free reproducible version of this figure.*

Providing Feedback

Feedback should not only focus on the positive elements of instruction, but also should provide direction for growth and improvement. Without feedback, teachers can't know where they stand in relation to the expectations for their performance. In helping turnaround teachers be successful, leaders should provide two types of feedback: (1) reinforcing and (2) developmental. We will take a closer look at each type.

Reinforcing Feedback

Reinforcing feedback lets the teacher know what he or she is doing well (and why) so that he or she can repeat the same behavior in the future. When providing reinforcing feedback, leaders should keep several important goals in mind.

‣ **Be specific:** Describe the positive or desired behavior you observe during the lesson. Focus on two or three behaviors, and make sure they match the priority instructional areas that you and the instructional leadership team have identified.

‣ **Be sincere:** Be genuine with your feedback while accurately describing what you observe. If you thought what the teacher did was outstanding or out of the ordinary or helped the students learn, let him or her know. If you noticed something the teacher did in the lesson that was not out of the ordinary or had a minor impact on the learning, you may choose not to mention that strategy in your feedback conference. Over-praising a teaching performance or giving excessive praise might make the teacher feel great at the moment but will soon be seen as insincere or even false praise.

‣ **Give immediate feedback:** Communicate observation feedback as soon after the walkthrough as possible. Feedback is more meaningful when given within a day or two of the observation.

‣ **Provide a rationale:** Providing the rationale for why a behavior is effective is an important part of the feedback process. A leader can provide rationale by pointing out the impact the behavior had on students or by sharing how the teaching strategy matches the school's expectations.

‣ **Encourage the teacher to keep working to implement the effective strategies:** This portion of feedback is often neglected because a leader may think, "The teacher must know to continue doing this." Encouragement is a powerful motivator for continued improvement and success.

Let's see how one principal, Lester Martin, uses regular feedback to help his teachers grow during the school-turnaround project.

> Principal Martin, the principal of Susan B. Anthony Elementary School, is working closely with collaborative teams and the school instructional leadership team to help teachers implement selected instructional strategies to improve student learning. One of the strategies that the instructional leadership team selected to use is problem solving in classrooms. Each teacher has designated a unit during the fall semester in which he or she will assist small student teams in solving a problem related to the content of the unit.
>
> As Principal Martin completes his walkthrough observations, he notices that Gina Mancini, a fifth-grade teacher, is doing an

excellent job implementing this strategy. Students are working in small cooperative groups developing plans to find ways to work with their community in cleaning up a local park. The students are on task, they are managing their voice levels, and they know how to get the materials they need to complete their projects, which they will then share with the class. Principal Martin also observes that while the students are working, Ms. Mancini walks around the room serving as a facilitator, answering questions, and asking students questions to help expand their thinking.

Principal Martin plans to hold a conference with Ms. Mancini to reinforce the teaching behaviors he observes. He plans a concise but meaningful conference to provide reinforcing feedback so Ms. Mancini will continue to implement the focus strategies and even improve them in future lessons.

During the conference, Principal Martin shares the following information.

- *He mentions that he observed her using several effective strategies, but for this conference, he plans to focus on one or two of the most significant strategies she implemented.*

- *He points out her effective implementation of problem-solving strategies when she asked the students to work on a local, meaningful problem to help them practice problem-solving techniques. He also points out that while he was watching, the students were working productively and kept their voices at a low level.*

- *He shares with her that problem solving will help students apply higher levels of thinking. He also points out that the low voice levels students used within their groups contribute to the focused learning culture she has established in her classroom.*

- *Principal Martin then recommends that Ms. Mancini continue to use both problem solving and managing student voice levels in future lessons and says that he will stop by her classroom in a couple of weeks to see how the student work groups are doing on their problem-solving activities.*

Principal Martin completes the conference in about ten minutes. He asks Ms. Mancini for any questions or comments she may have about his feedback. The teacher thanks her principal for stopping by her classroom and taking the time to share his thoughts about her instruction.

After the meeting Ms. Mancini feels positive and motivated to continue to work on implementing problem-solving and small-group work in her classroom. She is excited that Principal Martin recognizes her hard work and is looking forward to his next visit to her classroom.

In this example, we see how Principal Martin uses the power of reinforcing feedback to help teachers understand what they're doing well so that they continue to grow. If the principal didn't provide feedback, she might assume that he didn't care about what she was doing or wasn't interested in her success.

Providing reinforcing feedback also helps Principal Martin build a positive relationship with Ms. Mancini. This relationship will be important later when he may need to share improvement suggestions with her. She will be more receptive to hear and work on refinement strategies because of their positive relationship. We'll talk about this topic in more depth later in this chapter.

The completed template in figure 8.3 provides a worksheet for delivering a conference designed to reinforce and extend productive teaching practices. By writing out the plan for the conference, you will be better able to stay on track and make efficient use of your time. You'll also be modeling the same type of planning you are asking teachers to do on a daily basis in their classrooms.

Regular feedback in relation to teaching performance helps to let the teacher know what's going well in his or her classroom. It also helps to build a positive, professional relationship between you and the teachers. Reinforcing positive teaching strategies is one way to help impact teachers' professional growth while flipping or turning around a school.

There are times, however, when turnaround principals need to let teachers know when they need to refine or modify their teaching strategies. These modifications can be minor, and sharing refinements can be helpful. The needed changes might be complex where more in-depth feedback and suggestions are needed. We'll discuss the process of sharing needed changes in the next section.

Developmental Feedback

Developmental feedback is feedback that clearly identifies and explains an area or areas in which a teacher needs to refine or improve his or her teaching performance. By providing developmental feedback, a principal helps a teacher by breaking down what is expected of the teacher into learnable

Directions: Use the following template to plan and deliver a conference designed to reinforce and extend or enhance productive teaching techniques.

- Provide a specific description of the desired behavior or performance.

  In Tuesday's lesson, I noticed several strategies you used that were effective in helping students learn the concept you were teaching. During our conference today, I'd like to focus on one of those that was particularly effective: engaging all students in processing during the lesson. You did this three times during the lesson. At the beginning of the lesson, you asked everyone to think of their answer to the problem you had on the board for the students to solve when they came into the classroom. About halfway through the lesson, you asked the students to write down their answer to a question on a piece of paper. Finally, at the end of the lesson, you had the students share their thoughts in pair groups.

- Let the teacher know you are sincere with the feedback you provide.

  The strategies I'm giving you feedback on today are an important part of our school-turnaround plan and the goals we've set to improve student learning.

- Provide the rationale or reasoning for using and continuing to use the behavior you are reinforcing.

  The three examples I shared with you today ensured that all students were processing the information you shared in your lesson. As they processed, you walked around and made sure their answers were on track and focused. This strategy will help students be more successful since they are all on track and processing information during the entire lesson.

- Provide a statement encouraging the teacher to continue implementing the behavior.

  Since this was such a powerful strategy, I encourage you to continue to use it in the future.

- Let the teacher know you plan to follow up with him or her at a later date to support the teacher in continuing to implement the strategy or extend and enhance the strategy.

  I'll stop by in a couple of weeks and see how you have built on the participation and processing you started with this lesson.

Figure 8.3: Completed template for delivering reinforcing feedback.

*Visit **go.SolutionTree.com/schoolimprovement** for a reproducible version of this figure.*

parts, similar to what a teacher does with students in the classroom. This kind of feedback helps to ensure success for the teacher through careful articulation of what needs to be implemented and clarification on the incremental steps needed to implement it.

When providing developmental feedback, keep the following points in mind.

- ‣ Describe the behavior or performance issue that the teacher must focus on or change.

- ‣ Share examples (from the observation or experience) that illustrate the behavior or performance that must change.

- ‣ Provide the rationale for the change.

- State the new or desired behavior or performance to replace the problematic behavior. If helpful, share examples of what the new behavior or strategy will look like if implemented in the classroom.

- Check for understanding of the new expectations the teacher is to implement by asking open-ended questions. If the teacher can't articulate with clarity what's expected in the future, consider re-explaining them at this point.

- Share your desires and some opportunities to follow up to check on or support the change.

Let's see how a principal approaches a situation in which a teacher needs to refine a skill and the principal must provide developmental feedback.

Clare Robinson, the principal of King High School, is in the middle of one of her regular walkthrough cycles. During the cycle, she notices that a mathematics teacher, Ron Clark, has an issue with student engagement in his classroom. During the lesson, Mr. Clark does most of the talking. Some students appear to be listening, but others talk in small groups, have their heads down on their desks, doodle in their notebooks, and display other off-task behaviors. Principal Robinson checks her observation notes from previous walkthroughs and realizes that she has seen the same teaching behavior and lack of student engagement in previous visits. She decides it is time to hold a developmental conference with Mr. Clark.

To prepare for the conference, she identifies the issue she wants to address with Mr. Clark. She decides to focus on the implementation of student-engagement strategies. She develops a script for a conference in which she identifies the needed change (to help the teacher reduce his talking and get the students more engaged in the instruction), shares examples of the problematic student behavior in the lesson, talks to Mr. Clark about the rationale for implementing more engaging activities, and provides him with some examples of engaging activities he could implement.

In the past, Mr. Clark has brought up some of the difficulties he has faced in getting students more involved in processing during his mathematics classes. Principal Robinson knows it may be hard to implement engaging, active learning strategies in a mathematics classroom because of the individual nature of the content area, the way other teachers taught mathematics to students in the past, students' varied levels of understanding of the content, and the natural tendency of students in the school to want to just do only what they need to do in order to get a good grade in math. She identified statements of rationale to address his objections for more participation and several clear examples of ways he could increase the participation of his students to share with Mr. Clark during the conference. She also knows he will need considerable follow-up and support to guide him as he tries some of the engagement strategies in his classroom, so she plans to share opportunities for him to learn by attending a seminar on engagement, working with the school instructional coach, and observing some other colleagues as they implement student engagement in their classrooms. She will share these ideas plus find out from Mr. Clark what he thinks will be beneficial to his learning as well.

During the conference, Mr. Clark listens as Principal Robinson explains the issue and what she wants to see Mr. Clark do differently. After the explanation, surprisingly he expresses that he understands exactly what she is looking for and he believes he can be successful implementing the strategy in his teaching. He also shares that he is grateful for the opportunities for follow-up she has offered to help him learn to implement engagement in his classroom. He thanks her for putting together the ideas and helping him grow as a teacher.

In this scenario, Principal Robinson uses the developmental conference to actually teach Mr. Clark what she expects him to do and how he needs to change. Because she provided a very detailed explanation of what she expected him to change, and offered follow-up assistance, Mr. Clark clearly understands what his principal expects of him. During the conference, Principal Robinson focuses on observable evidence related to the teaching performance and observable behaviors; the areas of refinement or areas needing change are clear and specific. This is another attribute that makes the conference so helpful in communicating what needs to be changed.

Let's see how another principal approaches a similar situation with less factual clarity and causes a conflict.

John Newell, the principal of Hubbard Middle School, completes a round of walkthrough observations. Toward the end of these visits, he notices that Bill Long, a mathematics teacher, is doing most of the talking during the lesson. Some students are listening, but others are talking in small groups, lying their heads on their desks, drawing and doodling in their notebooks, and displaying other off-task behaviors.

When he gets back to his office, Principal Newell thinks about what he saw in the classroom. In checking his notes from past observations, he sees that this kind of teaching has become a pattern for Mr. Long. He decides to talk to the teacher about his behavior.

At the beginning of their conference, Mr. Newell tells Mr. Long he has a concern about his teaching; he believes too many students are off task, and Mr. Long needs to do something about it. The principal suggests that Mr. Long get the students more involved during the lesson. He tells Mr. Long, if students were more involved, there would be fewer discipline issues for the teacher to deal with and he would be able to spend more time helping students learn the required mathematics concepts.

Mr. Long becomes very defensive. He tells Mr. Newell that several of the more difficult students in the school are in his class and claims that it's enough work to keep students focused and on track during classes and that implementing strategies to get more of them involved really creates more opportunities for them to get off-track. He says he'll try but he can't guarantee he'll be successful. At the closing of the meeting he says that the best thing Principal Newell could do to support him is deal with these disruptive students when the teacher sends them to the office. The conference ends with no firm commitment to get more students involved (remember he said he'd try) and no follow-up assistance plan. Principal Newell now needs to find another way to help Mr. Long get more students engaged in processing information during lessons so they can improve their achievement.

In this scenario, we see how Principal Newell approaches the situation differently than the principal in the previous scenario. Principal Newell focuses more on what the teacher has done wrong than on the right way to use the teaching strategy. It's not surprising that the teacher became defensive given the confrontational way Principal Newell approached the situation.

In a similar situation, some teachers will appear to listen, nod their heads in agreement, then go back and teach the way they have always taught. Using a developmental-conferencing process to illustrate the needed changes increases the chances that teachers will grow, learn, and change their teaching practices. The developmental-conferencing process is an important tool that can be critical to the school-turnaround process.

Figure 8.4 is a template for conducting a developmental-feedback conference along with sample responses.

Directions: Use the following template to plan and deliver developmental-feedback conferences.

- Describe the behavior or performance issue that needs to change.

During the lesson I observed yesterday and in a few other lesson observations, I've noticed that you seem to be doing a lot of the work while the students are just listening or doing other things.

- Share examples that illustrate the behavior or performance issue that needs to change.

Yesterday when you were illustrating solving problems on the board, most of the students were sitting and watching you teach. When you asked the students for their ideas, only one or two raised their hands. The remainder continued to sit and listen but did not offer answers. At the end of the period when you gave students some time to work on their homework, many students who did not appear to be paying attention during the explanation of the concept all of a sudden had questions. You spent a lot of time re-explaining the concepts you originally taught the whole class and had very little time to help students who had more complex questions.

- Provide the rationale for the change.

It's important that we use strategies that help students to process information throughout the lesson. This increased processing helps them practice and learn concepts more effectively.

- State the new or desired behavior or performance and share examples.

I'd like to share a concept with you called engaging students in learning. This concept involves using teaching strategies that ensure students have to participate during the lesson. Some examples of strategies that fit into this concept include periodically stopping during note-taking and asking students to talk in pairs about what they've written in their notes, asking a question of the entire group and having all students write down their response, and asking students to respond chorally or signal answers simultaneously to you. In all of these examples, the students are processing and participating at the same time.

- Check to make sure the teacher understands the expectations for the new behavior or performance.

To make sure we are on the same page, share your understanding of the new skill I want you to implement and some examples of how it could be implemented in your classroom.

- Plan how you will follow up and support change.

To support you in using this new skill, I'd be happy to work with you as you plan future lessons. If you are interested, I can have the instructional coach share some ideas with you. Also, I'd like to stop by your classroom once you try to implement the strategy. Let me know when I could stop by in the next couple of weeks.

Figure 8.4: Completed template for delivering developmental feedback.

*Visit **go.SolutionTree.com/schoolimprovement** for a free reproducible version of this figure.*

We present reinforcing and developmental-conferencing processes as separate when, in reality, most principals simultaneously reinforce teachers for good performance and share ideas for refining for future lessons. They put these two processes together to help reinforce good teaching and explain needed changes in teachers' performance.

Figure 8.5 shows a process that utilizes both reinforcing and developmental feedback in one conference.

Directions: Use the following steps to plan your conversations with teachers.

1. Set a tone for the conversation. For example, "I'm glad we had a chance to get together and talk about your professional growth goals."

2. Overview the conversation or conference. For example, "Today, as we talk, I'd like you to share how things have been going for you in the last two weeks, what kinds of issues you have faced, and any questions you have for me. I will give you some places you can go to get your questions addressed. At the end of our conversation, we'll set up another time to meet later in the month."

3. Ask the coachee to outline his or her progress, situation, or question. For example, "Please take a few minutes to update me on your progress related to _____ over the last two weeks."

4. Provide feedback, strategies, or ideas to help the coachee address his or her progress, situation, or question. For example, "As you look for information on _____, you may consider checking in with _____. If _____ can't help you, ask _____ to give you some idea of who else may be able to provide you with the information."

5. Check to make sure the coachee understands the feedback and has developed a plan to move forward regarding the question or situation posed in the meeting. For example, "What do you think are your next steps in finding out more about _____? What questions do you have about the process?"

6. Set a follow-up meeting date. For example, "Do you want to set a time to meet later in the month, or do you want to just contact me when you feel a need to meet?"

Source: Eller & Eller, 2015, p. 67.

Figure 8.5: Conferencing template utilizing both reinforcing and developmental feedback.

*Visit **go.SolutionTree.com/schoolimprovement** for a free reproducible version of this figure.*

Even though the examples we present show principals engaged in observing and providing feedback, anyone charged with helping teachers to grow and learn can use the strategies. Mentors, peer coaches, and other teacher support staff have effectively used the tools. Consider sharing the templates in this chapter with these teacher support personnel.

In order for others (coaches, instructional leadership team members, department chairs, and other colleagues) to use the templates, use a more suggestive than directive tone. Since these colleagues provide assistance to their peers, you'd need to be careful so their advice isn't seen as telling their colleagues what to do. Since the principal has positional authority, he or she should offer the advice of support personnel such as coaches, instructional resource staff members, department chairs, and others to support their assessment of where the teacher needs to grow. If resource support staff are put in positions where they are asked to judge or evaluate their peers, serious damage to their collegial relationship could occur.

Tracking Progress

As you conduct observations, track the trends you see in the classroom. For example, let's say that over a two-week period, you have seen the start of class in fifteen classrooms. During these observations, you notice that most of the teachers spend a lot of time with management chores (taking attendance, collecting assignments, and so on) rather than immediately engaging students in learning activities. After reviewing your observation notes, you see that the first ten minutes are taken up dealing with these management activities. Over the next week, you decide to conduct more observations in other classrooms, focusing your attention on the first ten minutes of class. You see the same pattern in most of the rooms, except for three teachers who have developed successful strategies to take care of management issues without taking up much class time. In subsequent conferencing sessions with these teachers, you reinforce their abilities to take care of management chores without compromising valuable class time. For teachers who spend a lot of class time focusing on management issues, you provide developmental feedback to help them use the first few minutes of class more efficiently.

You may decide to plan professional development opportunities and activities to help teachers learn the skill of managing procedures without taking valuable class time. After this professional development, use observations to understand how teachers are progressing toward the desired level of implementation. For those moving along, coach and reinforce their efforts. For those not making significant progress, continue to work with them using additional professional development methods and feedback.

Turnaround principals use a variety of techniques and strategies to help them track progress. An example from one turnaround principal appears in figure 8.6 (page 168).

When using this continuum, periodically update it to visualize how implementation is moving forward. As more teachers are successfully implementing the strategy (and more are moving toward the right side of the continuum), the strategies you are using to help those not at the desired level of implementation should become more focused and personalized to meet their needs. For example, if several teachers are moving more slowly to add

Directions: Use the following template to track faculty implementation of priority teaching strategies.

Teaching strategy:

Handling management issues using minimal class time

Teachers Who Do Not Use Strategy	Teachers Who Have Started Implementing Strategy	Teachers Who Are Fully Implementing Strategy
Ms. Kramer, Mr. Wells, Mrs. Lansing	*Mr. Smith, Ms. Hanson, Mr. Lopez, Mr. Brown, Miss Sweeney, Miss Nguyen, Mr. Phillips*	*Mrs. Anderson, Mrs. Fernandez, Mr. Cox, Mr. Morrison, Miss Acosta*

What seems to be working to help teachers implement the new strategy?

Focusing on skills by collaborative teams, principal providing feedback on skill usage in feedback conferences, and mini-sessions for skill development scheduled before and after school

Ideas and strategies to consider to help the group make more progress in relation to the desired skills:

Focus the work of the instructional coach on the skill, begin to have peers observe one another, and provide more mini-sessions to help teachers learn more strategies.

Figure 8.6: Completed continuum template to track facultywide strategy implementation.

*Visit **go.SolutionTree.com/schoolimprovement** for a free reproducible version of this figure.*

strategies to their teaching, you may want to provide an opportunity for them to observe the strategy a colleague is using in the classroom, watch a video of a teacher using the concept while discussing the video with an instructional coach, or use some other learning strategy to help them better learn. Those who won't or can't implement the desired skill will require an intensive assistance or professional growth plan. Our book *Score to Soar* (Eller & Eller, 2015) provides more information about intensive assistance plans, their function, and other processes. In general, an intensive assistance plan breaks down an expected new teaching behavior into small, sequential parts. They also include timelines for the implementation, resources to help the teacher, and consequences that could occur if the expectations detailed in the plan are not met.

An intensive assistance plan is a good process because it lays the expectations and other elements out clearly. They help people who don't want to change because they raise the accountability. They help teachers who can't or don't know how to change by providing clear direction and resources to help them learn.

Providing Professional Development

Providing targeted professional development and learning opportunities is an important part of successful turnaround. Tailor the professional development content to address the needs you have identified through the teacher observation process, the school-improvement plan, individual teacher-growth plans, and other sources of information. We recommend the following types of professional learning opportunities for school turnaround.

Professional Development Workshops

Most schools have several professional development days built into their calendars. Rather than attending districtwide meetings and seminars, principals can design their own sessions to implement on these days. These customized sessions could include large-group seminars, small-group sessions tailored to teacher needs, and sessions led by internal staff members or district office personnel.

Mini-Sessions Before and After School

Another strategy turnaround principals have implemented with much success is mini learning sessions before and after school. In many schools, teachers are required to be onsite a certain amount of time before and after the student day. Occasionally, short, focused professional development sessions can be scheduled during these times.

Lunch Sessions

Some turnaround principals have found success in offering short, focused professional development sessions during the lunch break. In one school, the principal brought in an outside expert once each month to facilitate teacher learning. This outside expert focused on topics such as motivating adolescent males, successfully de-escalating conflict, working successfully with parents, and handling stress during the turnaround process. In this school, the principal made the sessions optional, but the topics motivated many faculty members to attend.

Peer and Instructional Coaching

Peer and instructional coaches can provide personalized and tailored professional development. They are helpful in the turnaround process because their assistance can be tailored to specific teacher needs. Peer and instructional coaches can help teachers better understand academic content, learn about new teaching strategies, and develop new formative and summative assessments, and can provide a variety of other resources based on teacher need. As these coaches spend time in classrooms observing teaching, they may be able to see areas where teachers need to make changes or implement new strategies. Coaches should approach each situation uniquely, providing a balance of support and the content each teacher needs to be successful. Having coaches observe teachers provides another set of eyes to help the teacher to grow and learn new strategies. Coaches should also keep in touch with the principal to ensure that the work they are doing is aligned with the principal's work.

Do not use coaches to address situations a principal should take care of him- or herself. Some situations are definitively the principal's responsibility, such as when a principal dislikes a specific teacher and balks at working with him or her, or is intimidated to work with a certain teacher, and so on.

Regular Faculty Meetings

Many principals have found great benefit in using regular faculty meeting time for professional learning rather than just providing information and announcements that can be handled through other methods such as email. One principal we worked with converted faculty meetings from information sessions to problem-solving opportunities. During each of the weekly meetings, teachers focused on either problem-solving student behavior, working to improve curriculum, discussing the results of assessments, or discussing progress on the school-improvement plan. Each weekly meeting started with an activity designed to reinforce a sense of being a team.

Collaborative Group Meetings

In many schools, teachers are members of collaborative teams (grade level, subject level, or vertical teams) that provide peers with ideas and support to learn about and adopt new teaching strategies. In one turnaround school we worked with, the principal established content-based collaborative teams to support teaching. These collaborative teams meet on a weekly basis to share the results of their assessments and to gain strategies and ideas to help them reach students who did not do well on their preassessments. These collaborative teams also help one another implement the priority teaching areas identified by the school instructional leadership team. Each collaborative team uses small video cameras to film themselves implementing the new priority strategies in their classroom. They bring these videos to the collaborative team meeting to show them and get feedback from their colleagues.

In other collaborative teams, members spend a part of their meeting time finding resources they can use to learn new priority teaching skills. Some of these examples include short videos of other teachers implementing these skills, articles outlining the new skills, commercial books, and resources that describe these new skills. Team members bring these resources to the collaborative team meeting to share with their colleagues. The collaborative team agrees to try out some of the skills and report back to the group on their initial efforts.

Delayed Starts and Early Dismissals

Some turnaround schools have regular delayed start times and early dismissal times for students. They use the time gained from schedule adjustments to provide teachers with time for professional development and learning activities.

School District Specialists

District specialists can work in the school to provide ideas, strategies, and coaching to teachers to help them gain new skills. These specialists can provide seminars related to the content, observe and provide feedback in classrooms, or serve as content coaches for teachers. Often, someone coming in from the outside can see the school and classrooms in an objective and independent way and help teachers to grow and change.

Floating Guest Teachers

Some turnaround schools have used guest teachers to provide time for regular teachers to participate in professional development during the school day. The principal develops a schedule where three or four teachers are freed up during a period for an hour to participate in professional development. While teachers are in these sessions, the substitute or guest teachers cover their classes.

Time During Whole-School Events

Assemblies and other whole-school events where the entire student body is in attendance are opportunities to involve the teaching staff in professional development. In some turnaround schools, a small number of teachers provide supervision for these events freeing up the remainder of the teaching staff to engage in professional development activities. Even though most of these events last less than an hour, it's possible to free up thirty to forty minutes of focused professional development time for the staff not involved in the assembly or event. Event supervision can be done on a rotating basis so different teachers are freed up on different dates. This allows people to learn with different peers and in different configurations. It's surprising to see how much professional development time a leader can capture using this technique.

Chapter Summary

A cycle of regular observation and feedback followed by targeted professional development provides a mechanism for school leaders to build the instructional skills staff need to ensure successful school turnaround. Let's return to our teacher from the beginning of the chapter, Val Hawkins, to see how she is progressing building new instructional skills.

> As the year progresses, elementary teacher Val Hawkins gains new ideas and skills to help her successfully work with even her most challenging students. Principal Norm Schultz visits her classroom and uses a balance of both reinforcing and developmental feedback during conferences to help her see what she is doing well and where she needs to grow. Val also participates in her grade-level collaborative team to gain new ideas and strategies. She also attends mini-sessions that Principal Schultz offers to help teachers at Everly Elementary School learn and implement new strategies.

> As the school year winds down, Ms. Hawkins is preparing for her final summative evaluation meeting with the principal. In this meeting, Principal Schultz shares with Ms. Hawkins how much she has grown during the year. She feels good about the progress she has made and the positive impact she has had on students, and she is looking forward to attending some of the professional development opportunities offered in the summer.

A school leader's ability to help teachers build capacity by learning and implementing new teaching strategies and tracking their progress should be at the center of any school-turnaround project. In the next chapter, "Successfully Managing Change," you'll learn ideas and strategies to help you manage turnaround and successfully navigate the change process.

Reflection Questions

As you reflect on the content of this chapter, answer the following questions.

1. How can school staff members work together to identify priority teaching strategies for teachers to implement in order to turn around student learning and achievement?

2. Why would a principal want to provide feedback using a reinforcing conference? What is the importance of specificity in feedback related to the successful performance of the teacher?

3. How can instructional coaches help their colleagues to learn new strategies to help them turn around student achievement?

4. Which of the ways that we presented to find time for professional development do you think might work at your school? What are the steps or processes you'll need to take or create in order to set up the strategies you selected?

5. How do you plan to track the progress your teachers are making toward learning the strategies they need in order to improve student achievement in their classrooms?

Chapter 9

Successfully Managing Change

Sophia Masters, the principal of Axis Middle School, has been working with her instructional leadership team. It is the first semester of a school-turnaround project. Since many of the strategies she and the team have identified for implementation are different from those the staff are accustomed to using, Principal Masters has started to encounter some resistance to the changes. She hears staff comments such as, "We never did this in the past," "I've never had to work so hard in my entire teaching career," and "I don't see how what we are doing is helping—the students still don't care about learning."

As Principal Masters reflects on the turnaround process to date, she notices that many of the negative comments fit a pattern. They all seem to focus on staff not understanding the impact of the changes on their personal and professional practice.

Principal Masters resists the temptation to scold or lecture the teachers when they complain or share concerns. She listens and makes note of their concerns. At the next staff meeting, she shares the staff's concerns and admits that their concerns show that they have needs in the change process that have not been met. These needs revolve around the concept of understanding how the new changes impact teachers both personally and professionally. She tells the staff that her top priority during the next few weeks is to address these needs.

In the example, we see how Principal Masters listens carefully to the concerns of her staff rather than brushing them off. She uses the information that she learns from listening to them to plan how she might improve the change process. Leading successful change requires constant monitoring and interventions to keep the turnaround process on track.

In this chapter, we'll talk about change, the change process, how to identify issues that can derail change, and strategies to mitigate these issues. You'll also learn how managing change will help you be successful in flipping your school and guiding it through the turnaround process.

Addressing Needs During Change

Early in this book we discuss the challenges a school and staff face upon being identified as a failing school. The initial reaction can be emotional and even hostile. For example, we discussed how people can go through a grieving process before accepting that, since the school is failing, it must be turned around. Similar reactions can occur as people experience the inevitable change that accompanies the implementation of new strategies during turnaround.

In *Working With Difficult and Resistant Staff* (Eller & Eller, 2011), we use the concept of frames of reference to describe the mindset that can make it hard for people to accept new ways of thinking typically associated with change.

People become accustomed to conditions and practices in the workplace. They see the patterns in processes, procedures, and organizational norms and values, and they use these patterns to help them determine how to work, think, and behave in the workplace. New workplace expectations, norms, or procedures change these conditions and practices.

Since the status quo is no longer acceptable, the old ways of doing things no longer work or are acceptable. New thinking and strategies are needed in order to deal with the new changes. Initially, staff may have difficulty accepting the changes and the new reality. They may try to return to older ways of operating or become resistant to new requirements and blame their discomfort on factors outside of their control. You may hear comments such as, "We could do well if we didn't have *those students*," or "Back in the good old days, parents always supported us. Now, they take their children's side every time."

Because the new ways of thinking and new strategies and processes are so different from what existed or was acceptable previously, they need time and support to be able to accept and function in the new environment.

The concept of frames of reference is helpful during the turnaround process. If you keep people's frames of reference in mind as you're going through change, you'll be able to anticipate some of their emotional reactions. Being prepared for these emotional reactions has helped many turnaround principals keep school change on track. Hord, Rutherford, Huling-Austin, and Hall (1987) identify stages of concern in their Concerns-Based Adoption Model

(CBAM). We've found these stages of concern to be a key concept for success in our own turnaround experiences. Being aware of and trying to meet people's needs during the turnaround process help everyone stay focused. They also let your staff know you care about them and want them to be successful.

The following seven stages of concern identify typical concerns that groups or individuals encounter during change. If the needs at one stage are not met, it is difficult, if not impossible, for people to move to the next stage.

1. **Awareness stage:** Having basic knowledge about the new expectations, practices, or strategies

2. **Information stage:** Possessing specific knowledge about the new expectations, practices, or strategies. Also, understanding specific details like the implementation schedule, the reasoning and rationale behind the program components, and other more detailed aspects related to the change or implementation.

3. **Personal stage:** Having an understanding of how the change or implementation affects them and the work they do in the school

4. **Management stage:** An understanding of how to operate or implement the strategies and techniques associated with the change or implementation

5. **Consequences stage:** Having a clear understanding of the impact of the changes, strategies, and techniques on the students and on student learning and achievement

6. **Collaboration stage:** Possessing a clear mastery of the techniques and strategies of the new innovation so that they can work with or collaborate with others in the use of these techniques and strategies

7. **Refocusing stage:** Having a clear understanding and experience in working with the new ideas, strategies, and techniques. Using this experience to begin to make adjustments or changes in these strategies and techniques to make them fit into the culture or practices of the classroom and the school. In other words, personalizing the program.

The concept of levels of concern has several implications for school leaders in turnaround situations.

▸ Understanding that there are certain levels of concern everyone will go through in relation to change helps leaders anticipate some of the issues they may face with their faculty so that they can proactively deal with these issues rather than waiting for them to emerge.

- ▸ Individual teachers may pass through the levels of concern at different paces.

- ▸ The first three stages of concern (awareness, information, and personal) focus on the individual. The principal may hear a lot of questions that include "I" or "me." Leaders can typically address needs in the first three levels through professional development (seminars, small group mini-sessions, and so on). Once the leader has addressed these basic needs, teachers need support, mentoring, and coaching to move through the next levels.

- ▸ It may be helpful to explain the concept of levels of concern to teachers at the start of a change or new implementation. If they know the stages they may go through during implementation, they may be better able to see their progress and understand that their feelings and concerns are normal during the change process.

Principals who are aware of and utilize the concept of levels of concern help their staff work through these levels in a productive manner. See how the principal in the following scenario utilizes the concept.

> Paul Grant, the principal of Evans Middle School, meets with his staff early in the change process to explain the changes that he and the instructional leadership team identified to help turn around student achievement at the school. During this staff meeting, Paul provides an overview of the needs of the school. He then has several members of the leadership team explain the strategies to attain the identified goals during the first year of the project. Paul explains that the turnaround process might feel emotionally taxing. He gives them a handout and articulates and describes the stages of concern that they might experience during this project. He also points out that the majority of the faculty will be dealing with the stages of awareness, information, personal, and management during the first year of implementation.
>
> As the school year progresses, Paul and the instructional leadership team offer a variety of professional development sessions for faculty related to the components of the school-improvement plan. These offerings include mini-sessions before and after school, collaborative team time focused on specific aspects of the improvement plan, and sessions involving release time by employing floating subs to cover classes so teachers get to attend short professional development sessions during

the school day. Each of the sessions is labeled according to the concern level the session is designed to address. For example, most of the sessions offered in October and November are "information sessions." This means they are designed to provide specific information about the processes and strategies teachers are required to implement. Principal Grant and the instructional leadership team start to notice some teachers are ready for management-level activities, so they offer some of these in addition to maintaining the information-related sessions.

In order to monitor the teachers' levels of concern, Principal Grant asks his mentors and coaches to determine the level of concern they observe in those they are working with. He encourages them to provide mentoring and coaching to address these specific levels. In faculty meetings, Principal Grant has teachers organize themselves into concern-level groups and holds discussions to identify their needs. The principal and the instructional leadership team take these lists of needs and use them to develop interventions. Monitoring and addressing the needs of the faculty is a lot of work, but it helps keep turnaround on track and a relatively positive experience at the school.

Principal Grant and the instructional leadership team understand the importance of levels of concern and their impact on the success of the school-turnaround project at Evans Middle School. They use this knowledge to monitor teachers' level of concern and implement the professional development and support teachers need to be successful.

Use figure 9.1 (page 180) to share information about the stages of concern with staff members and to collect information and encourage reflection. Column three provides space for teachers to identify their specific needs within each of the stages.

Managing Transition Periods

William Bridges (2009), in his book *Managing Transitions: Making the Most of Change*, identifies key elements for leaders to consider as they help people work through change, and he discusses the idea that the actual change is not as difficult as the *gaps*, or transition periods, associated with the process of change. Bridges contends that people's concerns are strongest when they are somewhere between the present and future way of operating. He provides ideas and strategies to help leaders manage these transition periods.

Concern Stage	Definition	Needs to Attain This Stage
Awareness	Having basic knowledge about the new expectations, practices, or strategies	
Informational	Possessing specific knowledge about the new expectations, practices, or strategies	
Personal	Having an understanding of how the change or implementation impacts them and the work they do in the school	
Management	Understanding how to operate the strategies and techniques associated with the change or implementation	
Consequences	Having a clear understanding of the impact of the changes, strategies, and techniques on students and student learning and achievement	
Collaboration	Possessing a clear mastery of the techniques and strategies of the new innovation to be able to work with or collaborate with others in its use	
Refocusing	Having a clear understanding and experience in working with the new ideas, strategies, and techniques and using this experience to begin to make adjustments or changes in these strategies and techniques to make them fit into the culture or practices of the classroom and the school; personalizing the program	

Figure 9.1: Template for explaining levels of concern and gathering group and individual needs.

*Visit **go.SolutionTree.com/schoolimprovement** for a free reproducible version of this figure.*

Bridges (2009) identifies three stages that relate to change: (1) endings (ending the old practice), (2) neutral zones (a waiting period while the new practices are being launched), and (3) new beginnings (the new way of doing business).

Figure 9.2 is an illustration of these stages.

Figure 9.2: Stages in managing the change process.

The arrows connecting these three stages are straight in the illustration in figure 9.2. In a real setting, the arrows may reflect a more turbulent path than a straight line.

Endings

In every change, something (a behavior, process, structure, and so on) ends. We must stop what we are doing in order to start something new. Endings can be a difficult process because people are being asked to let go of practices or behaviors that are familiar and comfortable. Leaders need to be aware of the trouble people may have in letting go of their old behaviors. People may need some form of emotional assistance in processing their endings.

Here are some strategies turnaround principals have used to help their teachers process endings.

> ▸ **Hold a ceremony or use a ritual to signify the end of a behavior that will no longer be used in the turnaround school:** These ceremonies help signify an ending, and open doors to new beginnings.

> ▸ **Allow teachers to discuss the positive aspects plus the challenges of working with the old strategy or process:** This strategy helps people see the old way of doing things in a more accurate way. Without an objective discussion, people tend to remember things in a more positive light, which may not be accurate.

Figure 9.3, the Sweet and Not-So-Sweet Memories activity, helps staff gain an accurate perception of the past practice.

Sweet and Not-So-Sweet Memories		
Directions: Name the project, program, or practice that is no longer going to be used. Once you have identified the program or practice, discuss the aspects (note them in the cells that follow) with the staff. Talk about some of their good memories of the practices, their not-so-sweet memories, and what they think they could add to replace the sweet memories in the new practice.		
Sweet memories or positive attributes of this program or practice	**Not-so-sweet, irritating, or somewhat negative aspects of this program or practice**	**Ideas or strategies to replace the sweet memories or positive attributes once this program or practice is gone**

Source: Adapted from Eller & Eller, 2006.

Figure 9.3: Sweet and not-so-sweet memories activity.

*Visit **go.SolutionTree.com/schoolimprovement** for a free reproducible version of this figure.*

This activity is helpful because it allows teachers to have a conversation about the strategy or practice that is ending but to also develop the connections the old strategy may have to the new idea or practice. The activity can be completed in small groups on individual templates or as a large group using chart paper.

- **Provide a transition schedule for ending the old procedure or process:** This allows people to go through some of the grieving stages in order to let go and move on.

- **Allow people to take something with them or keep something from the past:** Staff members might find it comforting to keep a procedural booklet or some other artifact that represents the process that is ending. This strategy helps them hang on to a little piece of the past while moving forward. In life, we do this when we keep a souvenir or other tangible item.

- **Use the past practice as a foundation for the new process or strategy:** By adding a new part to an older assessment strategy, people are able to retain part of what is familiar while moving forward with a new process or procedure.

The Neutral Zone

After the processes, strategies, and policies from the past have ended, the group enters a phase called the neutral zone. The neutral zone is a period of transition that the group remains in until the new processes, strategies, and policies start to take effect. This can be a dangerous zone because staff can become uncomfortable while they're in transition. It can also be a period of chaos because of uncertainties about the future. This anxiety is common when flipping a school and can derail a school-turnaround effort. If possible, leaders should try to manage the level of anxiety so it doesn't get out of control.

School-turnaround principals can manage transitions in the following ways.

- Openly discuss the neutral zone, its characteristics, and the emotions people may experience during this part of the transition process. If people know the neutral zone is coming, they can mentally prepare for it.

- Keep transitional periods as short as possible. Since people can feel lost during transitions, it's best to move through them without unnecessary delays. By thoroughly identifying the ripple effects related to a change before launching the change process, leaders are able to plan shorter transition experiences. Putting the plan in a visual format may help people.

- Develop temporary systems and processes during transitions. These temporary systems and processes help to establish a sense of direction and purpose during the transition.

▸ Manage the expectations during transitions so people don't become overwhelmed. For example, letting people know the transition process may consume a large amount of energy and temporarily reducing their supervision duties so they can concentrate on the transition lower anxiety and let them know you want to simplify their lives.

▸ Take the time to identify the winners and losers in the new change process. Winners are those who may gain something (more prestige, less work, and so on), and losers are those who will lose during a change (more work, having to take time to learn new strategies, and so on). Make sure you consider how you might work to replace some of the things that people stand to lose during the transition to the new processes and strategies.

Figure 9.4 (page 184) shows a template for the winners and losers in the change process tool. Leaders can use this tool to identify those who may benefit and those who may lose something in the change process.

Turnaround principals have found this tool to be helpful in anticipating difficulties they might encounter when implementing change and thinking through how they might be able to lessen the blow for teachers who might feel as though they are losing something during the new implementation or change.

See how this process works in the following example.

In the school-improvement plan that the instructional leadership team developed for Central High School, there is a goal related to improving mathematics achievement by providing more support to struggling students in introductory mathematics courses. This could be accomplished by having someone with a high level of content knowledge and expertise teach the introductory mathematics courses. Principal Janet Dougherty believes she might be able to secure a new teacher with the required competencies during the spring selection process.

When none of the candidates in the selection pool seem to have the required qualifications, Principal Dougherty decides to move one of her veteran teachers into the position. She immediately thinks of Lisa Durrant, the department chair and one of the most respected teachers in the school. Ms. Durrant has the content knowledge needed for the position, plus she would be able to manage some of the students' off-task behavior. Before approaching Ms. Durrant about the change, Principal Dougherty uses the winners and losers in the change process tool to identify

Winners and Losers in the Change Process

Directions: In a change effort or new program implementation, there will be people who gain something (winners) and those who lose something (losers). People who lose something as a result of the new program or change have the potential to become difficult and resistant. Use this template to help you identify the potential winners and losers in your change effort or new program implementation. As you list the winners and losers, place those with the most to win or lose near the top of the chart and those with the least to win or lose near the bottom of the chart.

1. Change project or new program implementation:

2. Details of the change required for the new program to be successful:

Winners	Losers

1. What are the most common aspects that those in the losing side of the template share? What are the trends on the winners' side of the template?

2. What sorts of resources can you offer to help replace the losses on the losing side of the template?

Source: Adapted from Eller & Eller, 2011.

Figure 9.4: Winners and losers in the change process tool.

*Visit **go.SolutionTree.com/schoolimprovement** for a reproducible version of this figure.*

the following possible losses for Ms. Durrant if she were teaching the alternate set of courses.

- *Loss of prestige of teaching higher-level courses*
- *The potential need to spend more time on classroom-management issues*
- *Loss of time due to the need for new planning and preparation*

Principal Dougherty knows that in order to minimize Ms. Durrant's resistance to the new idea, she has to find a way to compensate for the teacher's potential losses.

Principal Dougherty carefully considers all the issues and prepares for her conversation with Ms. Durrant by focusing on the following positives to balance the losses.

- *Ms. Durrant was selected for the move because of her outstanding content knowledge and classroom-management skills. The principal's view of Ms. Durrant's professional abilities will elevate her in the eyes of her peers.*

- *The new course assignment will allow some coteaching to take place, something Ms. Durrant has always wanted to try. Co-teaching would also reduce planning time and help Ms. Durrant feel supported and less alone in her new position.*

- *As a part of teaching the new introductory courses, Ms. Durrant will have the opportunity to select e-learning materials and technology tools for implementation in the course. She will also receive extra professional development opportunities related to the use of the new technology and instructional methods. Principal Dougherty knows these two aspects will be very motivational to Ms. Durrant.*

As Principal Dougherty explains the move to Ms. Durrant, the positive aspects she shares help keep the conversation positive. Even though Ms. Durrant has suffered some losses in the transition, she is excited about the positive gains that the change will bring.

In this example, we see how it paid off for Principal Dougherty to identify the teacher's potential losses before approaching her about teaching the new courses. Identifying winners and losers doesn't always prevent problems or negative feelings with staff members, but it is well worth the small amount of effort it takes to potentially avoid anxiety in transitional periods.

New Beginnings

The third stage in Bridges's (2009) transition model is new beginnings. This is the stage when changes are implemented. For most people, this is an exciting time. Even though it is exciting, keep the following in mind as you move forward with implementation during the new beginnings phase.

▸ Remind people of the rationale or impetus for the change.

▸ Continue to provide a clear vision of the outcomes or desired results.

▸ After you've articulated the vision, remind staff of the step-by-step details of the plan for change or implementation of a new behavior, process, and so on.

▸ Include short-term victories and celebrations. People like to take stock in quick gains and know that their efforts are celebrated and appreciated.

▸ Carefully and regularly monitor your progress toward your turnaround goals. Make regular adjustments to help keep the improvement plan on course.

Chapter Summary

Let's return to the principal featured at the opening of this chapter and see how she is managing the change process at Axis Middle School.

> *Throughout the school year, Principal Masters monitors the concern levels of her staff. She offers various professional development sessions to help meet their needs during the change process. Principal Masters holds several ceremonies or rituals with her teachers to help them process their endings as they move from old practices to new ones. She makes sure they are aware that it is okay to feel losses along the way, and she does her best to mitigate losses with gains.*

> *These strategies seem to be helping her staff positively work through the turnaround process. When Principal Masters notices that some staff have temporary setbacks or become frustrated or negative, she meets with them to address their needs. Because she has taken the time to understand and manage the change*

process, her school is making progress. The faculty meetings are no longer complaint sessions; instead, they are problem-solving and strategy-development sessions. Staff members have started taking on the major tasks of the school-turnaround process with great success. In many instances, the instructional leadership team volunteers to take care of issues before Principal Masters even has a chance to offer. The team and the school show tremendous growth as a result of their school-turnaround effort.

Managing the change process is an important consideration for principals who are working on school turnaround. This process must focus on the people in the school rather than on the technical aspects. In our experience, unsuccessful school-turnaround projects are often the result of leaders failing to manage the emotions associated with change. Whether the change is large or small, understanding the human element will help ensure success.

Reflection Questions

As you reflect on the content of this chapter, answer the following questions.

1. How can leaders fail in their turnaround efforts when they don't address staff needs?

2. How do both group and individual levels of concern affect a change effort?

3. How can principals of turnaround schools ensure they provide proper endings for teachers before moving forward with new processes or new beginnings? Why is it important to consider this when launching a school-improvement effort?

4. What is the value of celebration in the turnaround process?

Epilogue

Flipping or turning around a school can be rewarding work. It's exciting to see the things you and your team envisioned coming to fruition and working to improve student achievement. It's also gratifying watching teachers and students being successful in situations where they haven't been so in the past. In addition to learning more and achieving at higher levels, teachers and students look much happier. They develop a sense of pride in their work and in seeing the school's success. People who may have become discouraged in the past now brim with confidence as the school's culture of positivity and productivity continues to grow.

You as the leader can celebrate your hard work and success as well. It's because of you and how you have implemented the right kind of leadership that the school is back on track. We're sure you've experienced ups and downs over the course of your work, but it's all been worth it. Now comes the even more gratifying part of your leadership journey: building the structures to keep the school positive and moving forward and making the changes that have helped the school to be successful become a part of the ongoing culture.

Sometimes, leaders like you decide to stay at the school and enjoy the fruits of their labor. It can be fun to work with the school as it moves into the maintenance phase of the school-turnaround project. In many cases though, once they've helped flip one school with successful turnaround, principals move on to other challenges to support another school in need of turnaround. When this happens, the school benefits from the experiences the principal gained in his or her previous turnaround projects. Even though each school is unique and needs unique strategies and approaches, some of the core turnaround aspects transfer well from one experience to another. This is also true in flipping a real-estate property—the basic processes work for different projects.

A successful school-turnaround project flips the leader as well. Leaders should have a new sense of purpose with the confidence gained from guiding a school to success. You may have also changed your mindset toward adversity and change and increased your personal grit that we talked about in the beginning of this book. Your experience as a school-turnaround leader will benefit you as you take on additional career and personal challenges in your life.

We hope you found the strategies, techniques, and practices we presented in this book to be helpful; many others have traveled your path and found them to be beneficial. You may have completed your journey or have only taken the first step in the longer process of school turnaround. Either way, we hope you take what you've learned in these pages to make a great impact in the lives of your students.

References and Resources

Barr, R. D., & Yates, D. L. (2010). *Turning your school around: A self-guided audit for school improvement.* Bloomington, IN: Solution Tree Press.

Bridges, W. (2009). *Managing transitions: Making the most of change* (3rd ed.). Boston: Da Capo Press.

Buffum, A. (2017). *Taking action: A handbook for RTI at work.* Bloomington, IN: Solution Tree.

Collins, J. (2001). *Good to great: Why some companies make the leap . . . and others don't.* New York: HarperCollins.

Covey, S. R. (1991). *Principle-centered leadership.* New York: Free Press.

Duckworth, A. (2016). *Grit: The power of passion and perseverance.* New York: Scribner.

Duke, D. L. (2015). *Leadership for low-performing schools: A step-by-step guide to the school turnaround process.* Lanham, MD: Rowman & Littlefield.

Dweck, C. (2007). *Mindset: The new psychology of success.* New York: Ballantine Books.

Education Resource Strategies. (n.d.a). *Sustaining school turnaround at scale: Brief 1—Series overview.* Accessed at www.erstrategies.org/cms/files/112 -turnaround-brief-1.pdf on February 1, 2019.

Education Resource Strategies. (n.d.b). *Sustaining school turnaround at scale: Brief 2—Investing for sustainable turnaround.* Accessed at www.erstrategies .org/cms/files/1468-turnaround-brief-2-pdf.pdf on February 1, 2019.

Eller, J. (2004). *Effective group facilitation in education: How to energize meetings and manage difficult groups.* Thousand Oaks, CA: Corwin Press.

Eller, J. F., & Eller, S. (2009). *Creative strategies to transform school culture.* Thousand Oaks, CA: Corwin Press.

Eller, J. F., & Eller, S. A. (2011). *Working with difficult and resistant staff.* Bloomington, IN: Solution Tree Press.

Eller, J. F., & Eller, S. A. (2015). *Score to soar: Moving teachers from evaluation to professional growth.* Bloomington, IN: Solution Tree Press.

Eller, J. F., & Eller, S. A. (2016). *Thriving as a new teacher: Tools and stratagies for your first year.* Bloomington, IN: Solution Tree Press.

Eller, S., & Eller, J. (2006). *Energizing staff meetings.* Thousand Oaks, CA: Corwin Press.

Gladwell, M. (2002). *The tipping point: How little things can make a big difference.* New York: Little, Brown.

Goleman, D., Boyatzis, R., & McKee, A. (2002). *Primal leadership: Unleashing the power of emotional intelligence.* Boston: Harvard Business Review Press.

Hammond, Z. (2014). *Culturally responsive teaching and the brain: Promoting authentic engagement and rigor among culturally and linguistically diverse students.* Thousand Oaks, CA: Corwin Press.

Hattie, J. (2008). *Visible learning: A synthesis of over 800 meta-analyses relating to achievement.* New York; Routledge.

Hattie, J. (2014). *Visible learning for teachers: Maximizing impact on learning.* New York: Routledge.

Herman, R., Dawson, P., Dee, T., Greene, J., Maynard, R., Redding, S., et al. (2008). *Turning around chronically low-performing schools: A practice guide* (NCEE 2008–4020). Washington, DC: National Center for Education Evaluation and Regional Assistance, Institute of Education Sciences. Accessed at https://ies.ed.gov/ncee/wwc/Docs/PracticeGuide/Turnaround_pg_04181.pdf on February 1, 2019.

Hersey, P., Blanchard, K. H., & Natemeyer, W. E. (1979). Situational leadership, perception, and the impact of power. *Group & Organization Management, 4*(4), 418–428.

Hord, S. M., Rutherford, W. L., Huling-Austin, L., & Hall, G. E. (1987). *Taking charge of change.* Alexandria, VA: Association for Supervision and Curriculum Development.

Kotter, J. P. (1996). *Leading change.* Boston: Harvard Business Review Press.

Kouzes, J. M., & Posner, B. Z. (2017). *The leadership challenge: How to make extraordinary things happen in organizations* (6th ed.). San Francisco: Jossey-Bass.

Kowal, J., & Ableidinger, J. (2011). *Leading indicators of school turnarounds: How to know when dramatic change is on track.* Charlottesville: University of Virginia Partnership for Leaders in Education. Accessed at https://files.eric.ed.gov/fulltext/ED539555.pdf on February 1, 2019.

Kowal, J., Hassel, E. A., & Hassel, B. C. (2009). *Successful school turnarounds: Seven steps for district leaders.* Washington, DC: Center for Comprehensive School Reform and Improvement.

Kübler-Ross, E. (2014). *On death and dying: What the dying have to teach doctors, nurses, clergy and their own families*. New York: Scribner.

Leithwood, K., Harris, A., & Strauss, T. (2010). *Leading school turnaround: How successful leaders transform low-performing schools*. San Francisco: Jossey-Bass.

Maryland State Department of Education. (2011). *Teacher Capacity Needs Assessment (TCNA) attachments*. Accessed at http://archives.maryland publicschools.org/NR/rdonlyres/8337115A-1873-4429-969B-5196A8D1B1E7 /32050/2012_TCNA_Attachments_Booklet.pdf on May 22, 2019.

Meyers, C. V., & Murphy, J. (2007). Turning around failing schools: An analysis. *Journal of School Leadership, 17*(5), 631–659.

Miller, T. D., & Brown, C. (2015). *Dramatic action, dramatic improvement: The research on school turnaround*. Accessed at www.americanprogress.org /issues/education-k-12/reports/2015/03/31/110142/dramatic-action-dramatic -improvement on February 1, 2019.

Muhammad, A., & Hollie, S. (2012). *The will to lead, the skill to teach: Transforming schools at every level*. Bloomington, IN: Solution Tree Press.

Papa, R., & English, F. W. (2011). *Turnaround principals for underperforming schools*. Lanham, MD: Rowman & Littlefield.

Pierro, A., Raven, B. H., Amato, C., & Bélanger, J. J. (2013). Bases of social power, leadership styles, and organizational commitment. *International Journal of Psychology, 48*(6), 1122–1134. Accessed at http://dx.doi.org/10.1080/00207594 .2012.733398 on February 1, 2019.

Pink, D. H. (2011). *Drive: The surprising truth about what motivates us*. New York: Riverhead Books.

Raven, B. H. (2008). The bases of power and the power/interaction model of interpersonal influence. *Analyses of Social Issues and Public Policy, 8*(1), 1–22.

Schein, E. H. (2016). *Organizational culture and leadership* (5th ed.). San Francisco: Jossey-Bass.

Wheatley, M. J. (2006). *Leadership and the new science: Discovering order in a chaotic world*. San Francisco: Berrett-Koehler.

Winters, L., & Herman, J. (2011). *The turnaround toolkit: Managing rapid, sustainable school improvement*. Thousand Oaks, CA: Corwin Press.

Index

Working With Difficult and Resistant Staff
John F. Eller and Sheila A. Eller
Identify, confront, and manage all of the difficult and resistant staff you encounter. This book will help school leaders understand how to prevent and address negative staff behaviors to ensure positive school change.
BKF407

Score to Soar
John F. Eller and Sheila A. Eller
Discover how to guide and enhance the job performance of teachers in your school or district. You'll learn how to evaluate teacher effectiveness, use multiple forms of data for evaluation, and communicate evaluation findings in a way that fosters professional growth.
BKF625

Thriving as a New Teacher
John F. Eller and Sheila A. Eller
Discover strategies and tools for new-teacher success. Explore the six critical areas related to teaching that most impact new teachers and their students, from understanding yourself and implementing effective assessments to working confidently and effectively with colleagues.
BKF661

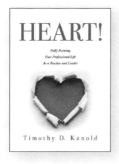

HEART!
Timothy D. Kanold
Explore the concept of a heartprint—the distinctive impression an educator's heart leaves on students and colleagues during his or her professional career. Use this resource to reflect on your professional journey and discover how to foster productive, heart-centered classrooms and schools.
BKF749

Solution Tree | Press

a division of
Solution Tree

Visit SolutionTree.com or call 800.733.6786 to order.

Wait! Your professional development journey doesn't have to end with the last pages of this book.

We realize improving student learning doesn't happen overnight. And your school or district shouldn't be left to puzzle out all the details of this process alone.

No matter where you are on the journey, we're committed to helping you get to the next stage.

Take advantage of everything from **custom workshops** to **keynote presentations** and **interactive web and video conferencing**. We can even help you develop an action plan tailored to fit your specific needs.

Let's get the conversation started.

Call 888.763.9045 today.

SolutionTree.com